Helen
& Charles Alexander

Helen Cadbury
& Charles Alexander

A love that embraced the world

Simon Fox

Marshall Pickering

Marshall Morgan and Scott
Marshall Pickering
34 – 42 Cleveland Street, London, W1P 5FB. U.K.

British Library Cataloguing in Publication Data
Fox, Simon
    Helen Cadbury and Charles Alexander
    1. Christian life
    I. Title
    248.4

    ISBN 0-551-01947-6

Text Set in Bembo by Selectmove Ltd, London
Printed and bound in Great Britain by
Cox & Wyman Ltd, Reading

Contents

Preface

Often in the history of the Church God has taken a tiny mustard seed of Christian faith and vision and made it grow into something great. This is without question true of the Pocket Testament League, founded almost one hundred years ago by Helen Cadbury, a twelve year-old schoolgirl, and now an international scripture distribution and missionary agency. The amazing growth and success of the League is clear evidence that God's anointing was upon it from the first, and this must surely have been because its aim was to bring people to faith in Jesus Christ by presenting them with the pure, unadulterated Word of God. This book is the story of Helen and her League.

Another major figure in this story is Helen's first husband, Charles Alexander, an evangelist and gospel singer of international fame in the early part of this century. Through his ministry, which took the world by storm and changed the lives of countless people all over the globe, the Pocket Testament League was put on an international footing. Alexander's name is not well remembered now, which is strange, because he must surely have been one of the most influential evangelists of modern times. I hope that this book will stimulate a renewed interest in him and his work.

Helen Cadbury is a biography, but I believe that it will not be of merely historical interest to its readers, since the success of both the Pocket Testament League and Charles

Alexander's ministry has relevance for the Church today. The League did not use gimmicks or clever techniques – it merely got the New Testament into people's hands and so enabled them to discover what God had said in his Word. The results were innumerable conversions to Christ and spiritual revivals in many lands. People simply read themselves into God's kingdom, very often without ever hearing a sermon preached or having anyone explain the truths of Scripture to them. The lesson here for the modern Church is a clear one: the Word of God is living and active and has in itself the power to save souls.

Charles Alexander also has something to teach us. He discovered that worship of God is not merely a sort of decorative optional extra in the life of the Church but is vital to its very existence. He found that by encouraging people to worship, he was able to bring the unsaved to salvation and Christians into a renewed love of and commitment to their Lord. In his great gospel meetings the Holy Spirit was able to work among the people because God was being praised. This same power of praise and worship has been rediscovered by today's Church.

In writing this book I have for the most part drawn my facts from the three volumes which Helen Cadbury herself wrote about her father, Charles Alexander and her second husband, Dr Amzi Clarence Dixon. In the few cases where Helen did not tell me everything I needed to know I had to do a little intelligent guesswork. Also, since I wanted to write the book in a popular, narrative style, I often had to exercise my imagination, while basing fiction upon fact. However, in every way I have tried to be true to the spirit of the story of Helen's life.

I would like to express my thanks to Patrick Bradley, Hannah Taylor, Mary Crocker and the many other people who gave me invaluable help by sharing with me their memories of Helen, so that I could make her character live in the pages of this book. My thanks also go to Geoffrey Simmons of the Pocket Testament League for all the research and letter writing which he has kindly done on my behalf.

Simon Fox
Brighton, April 1989

1

The Birth of the League

On 10th January 1877 the household of Richard and Emma Cadbury in Edgbaston, Birmingham, buzzed with anticipation. Emma was about to give birth for the second time since their marriage six years ago. Richard was in his study, praying for the safety of his wife and their child. Suddenly he heard the sound of an infant crying upstairs. Giving thanks to God, he rushed up the stairs and was met on the way to his wife's bedroom by one of his maids.

'Congratulations, sir,' she said, beaming with delight.

'Thank you, Mary,' he replied. 'Is – is Mrs Cadbury well?' he asked anxiously.

'Yes, sir, and the child too.'

'A boy or a girl?'

'A girl, sir.'

Once his wife had been made ready to see him, Richard entered her bedroom. He always experienced feelings of joy and wonder at the birth of one of his children. It was a miracle which never failed to amaze him.

His wife was sitting up in bed, holding the baby. Looking exhausted but serene, she smiled at him as he came to her bedside. He kissed her tenderly, took her hand lovingly in his own and gazed at the pink, wrinkled little bundle she was cradling in her arms.

'My dear, I don't know what to say – I'm so happy!' he whispered.

'So, we have another daughter, Richard,' said Emma, her joy and pride showing through her fatigue.

'We said we would call the child Helen if it were a girl, didn't we?' he said.

'Helen she is, then,' agreed Emma.

Richard bent over and kissed the infant on her forehead. 'Welcome to the family, little Helen Cadbury,' he said.

****

Richard Cadbury had married his first wife, Elizabeth, in 1861. She had given him three sons – Barrow, William and Richard – and one daughter, Jessie. Tragically, Elizabeth had died in 1868 and Richard, deeply shocked, had remained alone for three years. But in 1870 he had met Emma Wilson, the daughter of a widowed lady who had done much to help him care for his motherless children. Emma had been living for several years in Switzerland and when she returned to England and met Richard the two quickly fell in love. They were married in 1871, and the following year Emma gave birth to Edith, the first of four daughters. Helen was the second, followed by Margaret eighteen months later and Beatrice six years after that.

It is difficult to describe Richard Cadbury in a few words, so rich and larger-than-life was his character. But the most important fact about him was that he was a devout Christian. For generations his family had been Quakers and Richard followed the example of both his father and grandfather in expressing his faith not only by living a prayerful, godly life but also by helping his fellow men through charitable and philanthropic work. In addition to this, he was passionately concerned that people should put their faith in Jesus Christ as their Saviour, and so was energetically involved in evangelism. In his lifetime he came to be a famous figure in his native city of Birmingham and was loved and respected by both rich and poor alike.

However, while he took his faith very seriously, that did not make him a dour, sombre man. On the contrary, he had a rare talent for enjoying life and for enabling his family to enjoy it. He lived life to the full not despite his Christianity, but because of it. His faith in Jesus Christ filled him with such joy that everything he did was a celebration of the many-faceted goodness of God.

Emma Cadbury, too, was a sincere Christian. She had been an Anglican at the time she married Richard, but had joined the Society of Friends shortly afterwards. She loved children and cared for Richard's young family as if they were her own. So the Cadbury home was a happy place, full of Richard and Emma's love for God, for each other and for their beloved children.

Richard's father, John Cadbury, and his brother Benjamin had years ago set up a factory manufacturing cocoa and chocolate in Bridge Street in Birmingham. One of their reasons for choosing this line of business was their desire to encourage the drinking of chocolate as an alternative to alcohol, the effects of which were a very serious social problem at the time. In 1861 Richard and his younger brother George took over the running of the factory from their ailing father, and although there were financial problems for the first few years, eventually the business flourished under their care and the Cadbury brand name began to attain national and international fame.

So much did the firm prosper, in fact, that in 1879 they commenced the building of a new, much bigger, purpose-built factory in the countryside a few miles outside Birmingham. It was named Bournville after the trout stream known as the Bourn which flowed along the northern edge of the site. The factory was designed not only for the profitable running of the Cadburys' business but also with a view to the wellbeing of the workers, and was the first industrial complex to include such amenities as a cricket pitch, a football field, a playground, an open-air swimming pool, purpose-built housing for some of the staff and large and efficient catering facilities. In this, as in so many other ways, the Cadburys showed Christian love by caring for people's practical needs. They cared for their employees' spiritual welfare too, and each working day began with a voluntary time of prayer, which most of the workers eagerly attended. Both the Cadbury brothers were respected and loved by their staff for the genuineness of their Christianity.

Helen began her life in the home which her father and mother had set up at the start of their marriage in Edgbaston near Birmingham. This area was then on the fringe of the rapidly growing city and still had a rural atmosphere to it. The house had a pleasant garden which ran down to the edge of a wide, attractive canal with grassy banks. During winter the canal would often freeze over, and the children would have a wonderful time sliding about on the ice.

After Helen's father's business had moved to Bournville he decided that he should also move his home in order to be nearer to his work, so he took out a lease on the beautiful old house and estate known as Moseley Hall. It had been built in the early eighteenth century and had at one time been the home of the preacher-scientist Joseph Priestley.

The day of the move to Moseley Hall was one which the children always remembered with pleasure in later years. With mixed feelings of sadness and excitement they said goodbye to the house which had been their home and set off towards Moseley, leaving behind the attractive houses and gardens of Edgbaston. After a drive through the countryside which to the children seemed immensely long, they at last came to Moseley, with its village green surrounded by modest little houses and old-fashioned shops. There on a corner was the smithy, and up a street to the left was the square tower of the village church. Near the green was the entrance to Moseley Hall, guarded on either side by a gatekeeper's lodge. Their carriage passed through the tall, wooden gates beneath the shade of fine, old trees and started down the long drive, which wound its way between woods and fields and up and down hills. Finally, there before them was the house, with its grand portico of stone pillars.

Eagerly the children got out of the carriage and began to explore the fascinating old house. The cellars were much older than the rest of the house and some of them had actually been built and used as dungeons, a thought which both horrified and thrilled the young ones. And then there were the secret doors and passageways which previous occupants had constructed, possibly for sinister purposes or perhaps merely for their own amusement. The interior walls of the house were very thick and many of them had double doors, which meant that the children had plenty of hiding places to use in the games they played.

The views from Moseley Hall were beautiful. From the front of the house one looked down a large, sloping lawn to the waters of a delightful pond with a tree-shaded island in it. From there the eye rose up a grassy hillside to a thick belt of trees, above which soared the spire of St Anne's Church. The estate was teeming with rabbits, and the children often used to watch them feeding on the lawns. Not surprisingly, they soon nick-named Moseley Hall 'the Bunny House'.

The homely atmosphere of Moseley Hall was enjoyed not only by the family, but also by innumerable guests. All through the year the house and grounds were made available to people whose living conditions in Birmingham were difficult and who would benefit from a day out in the country. The guests included Sunday schools, men's and women's classes, mothers' meetings and Christian groups of every variety and denomination. Some of the larger parties were entertained in the fields adjoining the house and were provided with tents and booths in case of rain, while the smaller ones were invited into the gardens and the house itself. Every summer a great temperance meeting was held in the fields, which would in some years be attended by as many as twenty or thirty thousand people from all over Birmingham.

This was the happy and fascinating environment in which Helen Cadbury spent her childhood. She was surrounded by four brothers and four sisters, and so the family home was full of fun, laughter and sibling rivalry! From the start she had a strong, commanding character and tended to be the dominant personality among the children. She was also gifted with a good brain and did well at school. When she was fourteen the family moved to 'Uffculme', the beautiful house which her father had built just a few fields away from Moseley Hall.

****

When Helen was twelve years old she went with her father one Sunday evening to a gospel meeting at the mission hall which he had built in one of the slum districts of Birmingham. She sat at the back of the hall, watching the mission members as they brought in people from the neighbourhood – all of them looking poor and hungry, many of them the worse for drink. She was deeply impressed by what she saw that night. She knew that some of the mission people had once been just like the hopeless, shabby drunks whom they had brought to the meeting, and yet tonight they were sober and decently dressed and were singing the hymns with real joy and conviction. Something had dramatically changed their lives. Helen knew that it was the power of God.

The preacher finished his address, and then asked all those who wished to publicly confess that they were putting their faith in Jesus Christ to stand up. Helen had been brought up by devoutly Christian parents, but she now understood that that in itself did not make her a Christian. She knew that Jesus Christ had died on the cross so that she might have eternal life, and she now had to respond personally to what he had done for her. In her heart was a hunger – a desire to know God as her dear mother and father did. She stood up, along with several other people. Then the preacher asked them to go to a small room behind the pulpit, where mission members would pray with them. Helen felt a struggle going on inside her, but found the courage to step into the aisle. Hesitantly she went forward, feeling very alone and very young. There in the room was her father, talking with one of the men who had stood up in the hall. After he had prayed with him he came over to her at once with a tender smile on his face and a joyful light in his eyes.

'So, my dear, have you decided to give your life to the Lord Jesus?' he asked eagerly.

'Yes, I have, Papa,' answered Helen.

'Are you quite sure you know what that means? Do you understand why Jesus died on the cross for you?'

'Yes, Papa, I understand. He died for my sins.'

'Very good, my dear, very good,' he said, proud that his little daughter, at her tender age, had had the courage to make the most important decision in life. But then, from her infancy she had shown herself to have a bold, decisive character and had always been mature for her years. 'Come, let's sit down here on this bench and pray together.'

He prayed with her gently and lovingly, in no way belittling the importance of the commitment she was making that night, since he believed that a child's conversion could be every bit as real and valid as an adult's. As she sat beside her father as their carriage took them home that night, Helen felt a strange but wonderful elation welling up inside her. Although she could not express it in words at the time, in her heart she knew that God loved her and that through Jesus she had become his daughter.

Over the next few weeks she began to read the Bible avidly. The New Testament thrilled her to the core, and she grew to love it passionately. Her father watched her rapid spiritual progress with excitement and often spent time with her explaining the meaning of biblical passages which she found hard to understand. She soon discovered that the joy and peace which she had found in Christ were too wonderful to be kept private, and she was bursting to share her faith with others. She was inspired by the example of her father, who throughout his life had loved to witness to people about Christ. When she told him she wanted to share the gospel with her classmates he was very encouraging, but emphasised the importance of making it clear to the girls that what she was saying was not merely her own opinions and ideas, but was based directly upon the Word of God. Taking his advice, she started keeping a Bible in her desk at school, so that she would be able to look verses up in it whenever she needed to. Right from the start her hope and prayer was to bring her classmates to faith in Christ by sharing with them the plain, unadulterated Word of God.

One day she decided to pluck up the courage to tell one of her friends about Jesus and what he meant to her. When the day's lessons were over and there was no one left in the classroom but she and her friend Anna, Helen took the plunge.

'Anna,' she said, 'there is something I want to tell you.'

'What's that?' replied Anna as she tidied her desk.

'A few weeks ago my father took me to a gospel meeting at a mission hall, where a preacher talked about Christ. He said that to be a Christian a person needed to repent of his sins and receive Jesus as his Lord and Saviour. And that's what I did. I've become a Christian.'

'But isn't everyone a Christian?' asked Anna with surprise. 'My family and I go to church every Sunday – aren't we Christians?'

'Going to church doesn't necessarily make a person a Christian,' replied Helen.

8

Anna was puzzled. 'Well, this is all very strange,' she said. 'I've never heard our vicar say anything like that. I think what you are saying must be what Quakers believe. So I can't believe it, because I'm an Anglican, you see.'

'No, these aren't just the beliefs of Quakers – these are the things which every true Christian ought to believe.'

'But how can you be sure a Christian has to believe all that?'

'Because the Bible says so. Look, I'll show you.' Helen took her big King James Bible out of her desk. 'Look at this verse – Saint Paul's Epistle to the Romans, chapter ten, the ninth verse: "If thou shalt confess with thy mouth the Lord Jesus, and shalt believe in thine heart that God hath raised him from the dead, thou shalt be saved." Anna, can you confess with your mouth that Jesus is your Lord? Do you believe in your heart that God has raised him from the dead?'

Anna was doubtful, 'Well . . . I don't really know . . . I suppose so . . .'

'Let's look at another verse,' suggested Helen, full of enthusiasm. 'The Gospel of John is very clear. In chapter three verse three Jesus says, "Verily, verily, I say unto thee, Except a man be born again, he cannot see the kingdom of God."'

'What does "born again" mean?' asked Anna.

'It means becoming a new creation through Christ,' answered Helen.

Anna became very thoughtful. 'Helen, I think I'll have to go away and think about all this,' she said.

'Would you like to talk about it again tomorrow?' asked Helen.

'Well, perhaps.'

And so the two parted. That night Helen prayed fervently for Anna.

At the end of the next afternoon she and Helen had a long discussion about what it meant to be a true Christian. Anna had thought over the things Helen had told her the previous day, and she was becoming increasingly convinced by what her friend was saying. The obvious reality of Helen's love for Jesus had made a deep impression upon her. She was touched, too, by the fact that Helen was so genuinely concerned about her soul. And what she had said about personally receiving Jesus as her Saviour had struck a chord with Anna. She was growing out of the skin-deep, churchgoing religion of her parents and in her heart of hearts was searching for spiritual reality.

'So what must I do to become a Christian?' she eventually asked.

'You should repent of you sins and then ask Jesus to come into your life and be your Saviour and Lord,' answered Helen.

'Is that really all I have to do?' asked Anna, finding it difficult to believe that it could be so simple.

'Yes, that's all – to begin with. Then, you must live to serve Jesus, and other people.'

There was a short silence. They were both nervous – Anna about making this step of faith, Helen about leading her to do it.

'Will you receive Jesus?' asked Helen.

'Yes, I will,' said Anna, almost in a whisper. And so the two friends went to a quiet corner and prayed together, Anna confessing her faith in Jesus Christ. That day Helen went home from school brimming over with joy. She had no way of knowing it then, but Anna was the first of many souls she would win for Christ in a life dedicated to evangelism.

In the days that followed Helen continued to speak to her friends about Jesus, and her witnessing began to attract attention. One day Florence, another of her classmates, came and spoke to her.

'Helen, I've heard about what you're doing – telling the girls about Jesus Christ,' she said.

'Yes, I became a Christian a few weeks ago,' said Helen.

10

'I'm a Christian too,' professed Florence. 'I gave my life to Jesus last year. I want to witness for him like you do, but I'm too shy. I feel I don't know what to say.'

'All I do is tell people what the Bible says,' said Helen. 'I think that's all we need to do. God does the rest.'

Over the months that followed Helen and Florence prayed together regularly and witnessed to others about Christ, and as a result a number of their classmates put their faith in him. As far as possible they tried never to argue with a girl, but instead to present her with the plain truths of Scripture. They also made it a rule to speak to one girl at a time, when they could be alone with her. They wanted to communicate God's Word rather than get involved in debates. They often found that verses from the Bible were much more convincing to the girls they witnessed to when they were read out from its pages rather than quoted from memory. This method allowed no room for suspicions that they were making anything up or distorting the truth. Because carrying their large, bulky Bibles around the school would be impractical, they normally kept them in their desks. However, often their witnessing lost some of its effectiveness because they had to go and get their Bibles in order to quote from them, thereby losing the interest of the girls they were speaking with. This meant that they were able to witness only when in the classroom. But soon Helen and Florence had the idea of carrying small, pocket-sized New Testaments with them everywhere and using them whenever they had the opportunity, encouraging the girls who were converted to do the same.

After two years the number of Christians in the High School had grown considerably as a result of their witnessing and particularly through Helen's enthusiasm about Jesus and the strength of her conviction. Helen and the other leading lights among the Christian girls felt it was right to turn what had been merely an informal group into a proper society, with a name and a set of rules. They decided to call it the Pocket Testament League, since the carrying of a testament was what was distinctive about them. To be a member a girl had to pledge herself to always carry at least a New Testament with her everywhere, to read a portion of the Bible every day, to use the Word of God in witnessing to others about Christ and to join a Bible reading association such as the Scripture Union. The League would give one of the testaments which Helen's father had promised to provide to whoever wanted to join.

And so the Pocket Testament League was born and grew steadily as Helen and her friends went through their teens, so that when the time came for them to leave school, it had about sixty members. After their departure it carried on for a while, but then gradually petered out. How amazed Helen would have been if she could have known that this brave endeavour by a group of schoolgirls would one day be revived and would bring millions of people all over the globe to faith in Jesus Christ.

2

College Days

Helen grew up to be an attractive young woman with a shapely figure, abundant dark hair and a handsome face, full of character. She possessed a strong personality and had inherited her father's keen sense of humour and love of fun. At school she had gained a fine education and had developed a particular flair for music. When she was eighteen years old she went to Westfield College in London in order to complete her studies. This was a major upheaval in her life, since she had never before lived away from the family home. So while she enjoyed the intellectual stimulus of college life, at times she felt lonely, homesick and vulnerable. However, since she was gifted and bright she made good progress with her work and soon attracted the attention of the tutors. At the end of one of her days at college she got into conversation with her English literature tutor, Mrs Robertson.

'You wrote a fine essay on *Hamlet*, Helen,' she remarked.

'Oh, thank you, Mrs Robertson,' replied Helen, thrilled by this piece of praise. 'I find it a fascinating play.'

'You have a good command of English. Do you do any writing in your spare time?'

'Oh yes – I write stories, and I keep a journal.'

'Yes, keeping a journal is a very good habit – it trains you to put your thoughts and feelings into words. What sort of books do you read?'

'The book I read most of all is the Bible – I've read every bit of it several times.'

Mrs Robertson raised an eyebrow in surprise. 'Really? That's a considerable achievement in one so young. Why do you read it so much?'

'Because I love to read it,' replied Helen. 'It means a great deal to me, because it's the Word of God. Do you read your Bible, Mrs Robertson?'

The tutor hesitated. 'Yes – yes, I do, but I don't think I view the Bible in quite the same way as you do.'

Helen was immediately interested. 'Do you believe the Bible, Mrs Robertson?' she asked.

'Oh yes, but not quite in the way that you believe in it, I think.'

'But I thought that one either believed it or didn't believe it,' said Helen. 'You do believe it's the Word of God, don't you?'

'Well, it does rather depend on what one means by terms like "the word of God". I believe that there is a great deal of divine truth and wisdom in the Bible, but I don't think all of it is literally true. One simply can't accept all of it at face value.'

'Why not?'

'Well, for example, how can a person living in the present day and age take the beginning of Genesis literally? How can one believe that Eve was tempted by a snake? Snakes don't talk. Have you ever heard of a talking snake?'

'Well, no . . .'

'However, Helen, I wouldn't wish to try to change your beliefs. You must consider these things youself, and be true to your own conscience.'

Helen parted from Mrs Robertson feeling bewildered. She had encountered atheism and agnosticism at high school, but she had never heard an argument like Mrs Robertson's before – she had never met anyone who believed some parts of the Bible and disbelieved others, and who accepted it as being Truth in some

14

philosophical sense without necessarily being literally and historically true.

As the weeks went by Helen talked with Mrs Robertson on the same subject a number of times, and on each occasion she was disturbed and yet impressed by what her tutor said. Helen admired and respected her, because she was a highly gifted and intelligent woman, and increasingly found herself wanting to imitate her. And she began to wonder whether Mrs Robertson might indeed be right about the Bible. She was just as intelligent as her parents – probably more so. And she certainly had a wider knowledge of literature, philosophy and art than they did. Moreover, Mrs Robertson was a professing Christian and maintained high moral standards. So what right did Helen have to say that her views were wrong? Indeed, what if her own understanding of the Bible was erroneous? What if not all Scripture were meant to be taken literally? Perhaps it was true that her attitude to the Bible – and that of her parents – was crude and simplistic.

Helen returned to Birmingham after her first term at college in a confused state of mind. But it was so good to be home! She had greatly missed the warmth and love of her family. There was a hearty meal that evening to welcome Helen home, and later she and her mother and father sat together by the fireside in the lounge and chatted. Her parents were eager to hear all about her life at college. They took a keen interest in everything – her work, her tutors, her friends, her lodgings.

'And have you find a Christian fellowship to worship with, my dear?' asked Richard, stroking his bushy grey beard.

'Yes, Papa,' replied Helen. 'I've been going to the Friends' Meeting House every Sunday.'

'And do you try to win your fellow students to Christ, like you used to do at high school?'

Helen hesitated, not knowing how to explain. 'Well, no, Papa, I don't . . .'

It was obvious to him that something was wrong. 'Is all well with you spiritually, Helen?' he asked her gently. He had a very disarming way of asking questions. He could be very direct, but his loving concern for his children was always apparent.

'Well, Papa,' replied Helen, 'I have come across many new ideas at college – ideas which I hadn't heard of before.'

'What kind of ideas, my dear?' asked Helen's mother, looking anxious.

'One of my tutors, Mrs Robertson, sees things very differently to us. She believes that the Bible contains the Word of God – that it contains divine truth – but she doesn't believe that the Bible as a whole is the Word of God.'

'And what do you think of that, my dear?' asked her father.

'I don't know,' answered Helen quietly. 'I don't know what to think.'

He looked sad, but his big, expressive eyes were full of love for her. 'Well, my dear,' he said, 'whatever you may hear from your tutors and your fellow students, don't lose sight of the Lord Jesus. Don't forget that he loves you, and that he gave his life for you.'

'I won't forget, Papa – you know I won't,' Helen assured him.

He gazed upon her lovingly for a moment, a hint of doubt in his eyes. Then he yawned and stood up, stretching his limbs. 'Well, I think it's high time I was in bed,' he said. 'Sleep well, Helen,' he said, kissing his daughter on the forehead. 'Are you coming to bed now, my dear?' he asked his wife.

'Yes, I think so,' she replied, also kissing Helen goodnight. They went to their bedroom, and before they fell asleep they prayed earnestly together that their daughter would remain loyal to Jesus – a prayer that would often be upon their lips and in their hearts in the future.

The influence upon Helen of Mrs Robertson and the other tutors who thought the same way as she continued to grow during the two years that she spent at the college. Increasingly she distanced herself from her earlier beliefs and began to regard them as childish and not worthy of an intelligent person. The 'higher criticism' which the tutors espoused generally dismissed the traditional view that the Bible consisted of historically reliable writings, and as a result placed great emphasis on finding moral truths rather than factual certainties within its pages. Helen came to feel that her parents' spirituality – including their belief in Christ's resurrection and the miracles which he performed – was founded upon an inadequate basis of historical fact. She increasingly took the view that while it was debatable whether or not Christ had risen from the dead, it was indisputable that he had given the most sublime moral teaching that had ever passed the lips of a human being.

She felt exhiliarated to be free from what she now looked upon as the bondage of ignorance, and yet she was not altogether content. The strong, joyful faith of her parents – particularly that of of her father – disturbed her. What bothered her most of all was the fact that although Richard's life was so radiantly full of Christian love and thought for the wellbeing of others, he nevertheless had an unshakeable belief in the truth of the Bible's stern statements about sin and God's punishment of it. Also, he could not be persuaded that there was any means of spiritual salvation except the atoning death of Christ. He constantly referred to 'the precious blood of Christ' and its ability to cleanse from sin. How, asked Mrs Robertson and the other tutors, could the blood of a man – even the very best of men – shed almost two thousand years ago have any consequence in the lives of people in the modern age? How could any intelligent, sensitive person believe that salvation lay in substitutionary sacrifice, a primitive religious idea as old as the world itself? And yet Helen's father believed

17

in it, and she had never met a more loving person than he. At times she found herself despising her mother and father for what she saw as their narrow-mindedness, but then she felt remorse for thinking that way about such loving parents. At times she almost wished they would take a more stern attitude and insist that she see things the way they did – then she would have a good excuse for rebelling against them and rejecting their beliefs. But they did not try to pressurise or manipulate her in any way. They let her know, simply and honestly, that they were unhappy about her views, but they made it clear that they still loved her as much as ever.

Helen had a fine singing voice and was becoming an accomplished pianist and violinist, so after finishing her college career she went to Germany for a few months to study music, an experience which took her yet further away from the love for Jesus she had once had. She immersed herself in the arts, and before long she began to want to go to see operas, even though her parents had always warned her against them, since they believed them to have a harmful moral effect. Although she had abandoned many of her old beliefs, she still held onto her Christian morality and believed she should honour her parents, so before attending any operas she wrote to ask their permission. Her father replied:

Of course, you are of an age to judge for yourself on such matters, and neither mother or I wish to dictate or lay down our will against your well-considered judgement. Nor do I know sufficient of the surroundings and character of such entertainments to go into any details. I have been very happy without anything of the kind, and so far our children have not only had happy lives, but lives which have been untainted with the fascination that often draws young girls into worldly life and associations. I want you to feel that we both have every confidence in *you*, and are quite sure that you will not enter into anything that you know you cannot ask God's blessing upon. This is our safeguard, if we are honest to our convictions and make God's written word our rule of conduct. I think we realise your reasons on the question of the opera as the means of hearing musical talent, and of education, and do not for a moment dispute it. Make it a matter of earnest prayer, and God will guide you aright, and then rest assured that we shall not judge you. May the Lord bless you, my darling, with his richest blessings, and make you still a blessing to others.

With dearest love from us all, your affectionate father.

Helen found this letter totally disarming. She had expected her father to forbid her to go to the operas and had prepared herself to feel duly resentful. But instead of forbidding her he had gently and lovingly appealed to her better judgement. Once again the strength and reality of her father's Christian love moved and disturbed her.

However, despite her parents' views on the matter, Helen persuaded herself that it was right for her to attend the operas, and began to do so. Her passionate love of music for music's sake continued to grow and her love for Christ became increasingly cool. Indeed, a real indifference towards spiritual things started to creep over her. She rarely went to church and never found time for private prayer.

After her stay in Germany Helen spent her time helping her mother run the family home, while also devoting many of her hours to her beloved music. She was uncertain what she should do with her life in the long term. Should she marry soon, or should she try to develop a career in music?

Meanwhile her father, who for years had been a keen Egyptologist, had arranged a three-month-long trip for the family to Egypt and Palestine, and they spent the whole of January 1899 in excited preparation. Even though Helen had been to Egypt with her father just a couple of years before, she was looking forward to this trip, since a traveller in the East could never run out of fascinating things to see.

On the evening before they were due to leave, a family dinner party was held at 'Uffculme', at which the entire Cadbury clan gathered. Those who were going on the great expedition were in high spirits, and those who were staying behind found their excitement infectious. Richard had to leave the party early in order to attend a Gospel Temperance Mission meeting, but on returning home that night he threw his hat in the air and said with a happy laugh, 'And now for a long holiday!'

On the afternoon of the following day, 2nd February, the family gathered once again at New Street Station in Birmingham. There were seven travellers altogether: Richard, his wife, their daughters Edith, Helen, Margaret and Beatrice and Edith's husband Arnold. The remnant of the tribe waved enthusiastically as the train left the platform. The travellers crossed France and Italy, then sailed from Brindisi to Port Said in Egypt. There followed a long day's rail journey along the Suez Canal to Ismailia and across the desert to Cairo. They saw the sights of that city and visited the Pyramids and the Sphinx. Then they travelled southward up the Nile, visiting ancient ruined cities and temples along the way.

On this holiday Helen's father was even more full of fun, good humour and care for others than he usually was. It was as if the deepest part of him knew that his end was near and was urging him to live life to the full in his final weeks. He seemed to possess an extraordinary magnetic quality which attracted all sorts of people to him. One English traveller they met, who had apparently spent his entire life doing nothing but travel and pursue various sports, followed Richard about everywhere. As they were about to go their separate ways he whispered to Richard's wife, 'Your husband is the jolliest old chap I've ever met!'

When they returned to Cairo Richard noticed that he had developed a sore throat, and Helen complained of similar symptoms. For a few days both of them were very ill. Richard had planned that the family should spend the next part of the holiday in Palestine, but it was now doubtful whether he and Helen were well enough for the journey. However, a doctor diagnosed the problem as the common complaint known as 'Nile throat', and agreed that it was safe for the invalids to travel by boat to Palestine, since the fresh air of the trip would be good for them. But it so happened that the steamer they sailed upon was carrying a cargo of cement, the dust from which aggravated Richard and Helen's condition.

From Jaffa on the coast of Palestine they drove by carriage to Jerusalem. Richard displayed his usual Christlike care for others, even though the conditions were uncomfortable and wearying and his throat was so sore that he could eat nothing. Helen's health was beginning to improve by the time they reached Jerusalem, on the evening of Saturday 18th March, but now Beatrice also had a bad throat. The family stayed in a comfortable hotel and the invalids received very thorough medical treatment, because the illness had now been diagnosed as diphtheria.

By the following Tuesday they all seemed better, although Richard was weaker than his daughters. That evening they made plans to spend the next month seeing the historic sights of the Holy Land. At bedtime Helen's parents briefly read the Bible and prayed together as usual, and then fell asleep. But Richard's prayers were to be his last words. During the night Emma tried to rouse him so that she could give him the dose of medicine he was due to take, but he would not awaken. She realised then that he was not asleep but unconscious. She spent the rest of the night sitting beside him anxiously.

Then, in the small hours of the morning, she saw him open his eyes. They brightened with what seemed to be joyful surprise. Then his face took on an expression of rapture and he suddenly sat up with his hands lifted as if in adoration. He appeared to be gazing at a heavenly sight that was hidden from the eyes of his wife. Emma knew what she was witnessing, and with mingled love and reverence watched as the life faded from her husband's face and his body slumped back against the pillows. Richard Cadbury, who had always lived his life ready to meet his Saviour face to face, had finally experienced that longed-for encounter.

To begin with the family was in a numbed state of shock. How could Richard, who had seemed so full of life and vitality these past few weeks, suddenly pass away? How could they begin to conceive of living without his warm, loving, jovial presence among them? Such was his wife's sorrow that she was almost struck dumb.

They knew that thousands of people would wish to pay their last respects to Richard, who by his charity and good will towards his fellow man had won vast numbers of friends, so it was agreed that the funeral should be held in England. The family made the dismal journey home, bearing with them the embalmed body of their love one. On April 7th they reached 'Uffculme' in a state of weary grief. The household servants were just as striken with sorrow as the family, because Richard had been a dear friend to them as well as a master.

During the sixteen days since his death hundreds of messages of condolence had been sent. Richard Cadbury was mourned by great numbers of people of diverse religious persuasions and social classes, both in Britain and abroad. He had always been a larger-than-life figure in Birmingham, and his native city grieved deeply now. One local newspaper spoke of 'a profound sense of sorrow amongst all classes' and another remarked that 'it is impossible to overestimate the gravity of the loss the city has sustained'.

The funeral was held the day after the family's return to England at Lodge Hill Cemetery in Selly Oak. About ten thousand people from Birmingham and much further afield gathered to say a final farewell to Richard Cadbury. Some came in carriages while others came on foot, despite the bad weather. It was a bitterly cold day, with dense cloud cover and frequent hailstorms, but now and then a few shafts of sunshine would pierce the gloom. The grave was at the top of a hillside commanding fine views of the city and of the Lickey and Clent Hills. Present at the graveside were the Bishop of Coventry and Alderman White of Birmingham, who had been a friend of Richard's for many years.

At about three o'clock perfect silence fell over the great crowd of mourners as the Cadbury family, bearing the coffin, drew near. As the simple funeral ceremony began, conducted according to the tradition of the Society of Friends, an icy wind blew and a shower of hail fell. Helen watched as the coffin was gently lowered into the grave, salty tears stinging her eyes and cheeks. Then the clouds parted briefly and the mourners were bathed in bright sunshine as they sang the hymn, *Peace, perfect peace*. Just at that moment a lark that had been nearby rose up into the sky, seemingly from the grave itself, greeting the sun with its song.

Then Alderman White read from Paul's First Letter to the Corinthians: 'Behold, I show you a mystery: We shall not all sleep, but we shall all be changed, in a moment, in the twinkling of an eye, at the last trump: for the trumpet shall sound, and the dead shall be raised incorruptible, and we shall be changed. For this corruptible must put on incorruption, and this mortal must put on immortality. So when this corruptible shall have put on incorruption, and this mortal shall

23

have put on immortality, then shall be brought to pass the saying that is written, "Death is swallowed up in victory."

'O death, where is thy sting? O grave, where is thy victory? The sting of death is sin; and the strength of sin is the law. But thanks be to God, which giveth us the victory through our Lord Jesus Christ.' His voice trembled with grief, but grew stronger as he continued: 'Some of us have been helped by the life of our departed brother – some of us have been helped by his words, some of us by his prayers, when he seemed to come into such close union with his God and Father. We are suffering from his loss, but we can rejoice for him.' Again his voice faltered. 'The secret of his fruitful life was his abiding in Jesus Christ. May we who are left for a little longer likewise abide in him and walk in still closer union with each other.'

There were other prayers and a final hymn, and then the Bishop pronounced the benediction. The mourners quietly went away, saddened by Richard Cadbury's departure and yet encouraged by the thought that he was now in the presence of God.

During the carriage journey home Helen began to feel the full weight of bereavement falling upon her. Previously she had been too stunned to really appreciate the loss they had all suffered, but now that her father's body had actually been laid to rest, the pain was starting to set in. She realised more than ever before that her father had always been a pillar of strength to her, and now that he was gone (could he *really* be gone?) she felt that her life was like a building struck by an earthquake, tottering and about to collapse. Where now would she get the strength she needed?

Margaret and Beatrice sat opposite her in the car, weeping quietly. Beside her was her mother, her cheeks streaked with tears. Compassion for her welled up in Helen's heart, for she knew her mother's grief must be far greater than her own. Mother and daughter exchanged glances full of love and shared sorrow and held each other's hand, both of them seeking and offering comfort. There and then Helen resolved that no matter how she felt, no matter what the future held for her, she would do all she could to console her beloved mother.

3

Grief and Joy

Helen was taking a walk in the gardens of 'Uffculme'. She had a clear view of Moseley Hall, the family's former home, which lay just a few fields away. It was always a graphic reminder of her happy childhood days, and of her dear father, who had passed away nearly five years ago. Helen wondered what the impending new year – 1904 – would hold in store for her. She knew what she most wanted to happen: she wished to meet the man who was to be her husband. A chilly gust of wind interrupted her thoughts. She shivered and moved on in order to keep warm.

Since her father had died she had lived at home with her mother. To Helen, looking after her had been a sacred trust and one which had brought her great joy. She had also spent time with her working for the slum mission which her father had founded and in which she herself had become a Christian all those years ago. At first she had done this mostly to comfort her mother, but as time went by she had begun to feel real enthusiasm for the work, because by degrees her faith in God was returning to her. In the face of such a soul-rending experience as the death of her father, the sophisticated views she had adopted at college had simply evaporated. Of what comfort was a faith which was always questioning and never believing, which would accept nothing in the Bible at face value, when confronted with the shattering trauma of bereavement? Just as she had mourned her father and had wished that he were still with his family, so Helen had mourned his strong, joyful faith in Christ. She had needed the certainty and the peace which he had had, and so she had begun to pray and read the Bible again. Once more Christ had become real to her, and she had begun to wonder how she could ever have lived without him, without the daily experience of his presence in her life. What kind of spell had her college tutors cast over her? Even now she still had many doubts, particularly about the authority of the Bible, but she was determined never again to succumb to the slow spiritual death which had crept over her during her college days. She would never again shut the Lord Jesus out of her life.

Helen walked on, over the gently undulating grounds. She passed through the rockeries which had been a special delight to her father. He had spent many happy hours planning them and had often helped the gardeners as they laid them out. From the brow of the hill upon which the house stood Helen looked down towards the two ponds which her father had made, transforming what had been a neglected piece of marshy ground into a place of beauty. She passed over the rustic bridge spanning the little stream which ran between the pools.

Although Helen knew she had much to be grateful for, she was dissatisfied with her life. Although she and her mother were the greatest of friends, she still felt lonely sometimes. The family home, which had once been full to overflowing, was now quiet and empty. Her three brothers and two of her sisters, all older than her, were now married, while her two younger sisters, Margaret and Beatrice, were away from home – Margaret in Italy and Beatrice at college in London. But Helen also felt another, deeper loneliness which not even the presence of her entire family would have been able to cure. She was nearly twenty-seven years old, and she was still single. She very much wanted to marry, but no man she had met had been sufficiently appealing, although quite a number had shown an interest in her. Perhaps no man could be quite good enough in her eyes because none she had met were of the same spiritual stature as her beloved father. But then, who could measure up to him? There could be no more than a mere handful of Christian young men in the whole country who could be compared to him, and she felt she was unlikely to ever marry any of them. She sighed. Perhaps she was destined to become an old maid. Perhaps that was the price she had to pay for having such a wonderful father.

However, although she could not foresee it at the time, she was destined for a very special marriage. For in many ways she was a highly remarkable young woman. Although at one time it had been in abeyance, her Christian faith and commitment was of a high calibre and would be greatly used by God in the future. She also had a powerful character, seemingly boundless energy, a sharp mind and a great capacity for loving others. The man who married her would be greatly blessed.

She went indoors after a while and joined her mother for a cup of tea. 'My dear, look at this in the newspaper!' she said as Helen entered the lounge.

'What is it, mother?' asked Helen.

'Mr Alexander and Dr Torrey are coming here – to Birmingham!'

'Really? How exciting!'

Charles McCallon Alexander and Reuben Archer Torrey were American evangelists who had been all around the world with the gospel message. In the previous two years they had toured North America, Australia, New Zealand and India and had finally come to Great Britain, holding campaigns in London, Edinburgh, Aberdeen, Dundee, Belfast, Manchester and Liverpool. Everywhere they went they created a big stir and attracted great crowds. Alexander was a superb singer and possessed an exceptional gift for leading crowds in enthusiastic worship, and Torrey was an outstanding preacher who presented the gospel in a challenging, compelling way. Vast numbers of people all over the world had put their faith in Jesus as a result of the work of these two men. And now they were coming to Birmingham!

'Let me see the newspaper, mother!' said Helen. She sat down on the couch beside her. 'Where is it being held?'

'In Bingley Hall. It says here that anyone who wishes to help with the campaign should apply in writing to the address below.'

So Helen and her mother wrote without delay, offering their services as cousellors to those at the meetings who wanted to become Christians.

At the opening meeting of the Torrey-Alexander mission in Birmingham on the evening of Sunday 17th January Bingley Hall was packed with thousands of people. At the far end was a crimson-carpeted dais, and behind this was a great choir, composed of men and women from the Birmingham churches. On the wall behind them was an enormous banner bearing the slogan *Get right with God*, which was the heart of the Torrey-Alexander message. The good-humoured crowd buzzed with excitement as they waited for the meeting to begin.

Then, at eight o'clock, a group of people emerged from one of the hall's side rooms made their way swiftly down one of the aisles towards the dais. Immediately the crowd, throwing aside their English reserve, applauded loudly. Charles Alexander – a tall, slender young man with a strong, happy face and hair that was thinning on top – stepped up onto the platform while his accompanist sat down at his piano and Dr Torrey took a seat nearby.

Alexander smiled broadly and raised his hands. The crowd quietened instantly. 'Good evening, ladies and gentlemen!' he said, his strong voice with its Southern accent carrying clearly to all corners of the hall. 'Thank you very much for your warm welcome! It's a great pleasure to be here in Birmingham, England, tonight. Let's all worship the Lord together, because he is worthy of all worship, praise and glory. Let's begin our evening by singing a song called *The Glory Song*. It's on page twenty-two of your hymnals.'

The crowd found the song in their books and murmured with anticipation, having heard how it had set Australia and New Zealand alight. The pianist played a few preliminary bars, and then the choir sang the chorus:

> *Oh, that will be glory for me,*
> *Glory for me, glory for me,*
> *When, by His grace, I shall look on His face,*
> *That will be glory, be glory for me!*

Now Alexander made one gallery of the great hall after another sing it. Each time the singing grew more bold and enthusiastic as the people got the hang of the tune. Then the choir sang the first verse, and various parts of the crowd were made to sing the others. Finally Alexander called out '*Everybody!*' and the entire hall burst into joyful song, singing the hymn right through. It was a thrilling start to the evening. Later they sang other songs, hymns and choruses, such as *There's Power in the Blood, Never Lose Sight of Jesus, Loyalty to Christ* and *Shall We Gather at the River*? They were melodious and rhythmic and had clear, powerful words which encouraged and challenged the people as they sang.

Helen was bowled over by Alexander at once, as everyone was. His tenor voice was beautiful, and his ability to lead the great crowd in worship was extraordinary. He seemed to have the people in the palm of his hand and could make them do anything he wanted them to. He could make them jubilant with a song about victory over sin and death through Christ, or he could make them reverent and adoring as they sang about the sacrifice which Jesus had made for them on the cross. He was like a man playing a mighty musical instrument, composed of thousands of human voices.

30

Alexander, with his silver voice, ready wit and charming smile, knew exactly how to use his instrument to get the best results for his heavenly Master. His hands had a remarkable power over the crowd. The voices of thousands were controlled by their expressive movements – sometimes subtle, sometimes powerful and dramatic.

It was transparently obvious to Helen that here was a man who did not merely possess outstanding musical gifts, but who had been called by God to his ministry of gospel song and was filled with the power of the Holy Spirit. He was able to direct an auditorium full of people in such an amazing way partly through natural talent and the magnetism of his personality, but there was more to it than that. People were impressed by him because, whether they realised it or not, through him they felt the reality of God in a very tangible, exciting way. Alexander exuded Christian love and joy and somehow radiated the very presence of God. Helen was reminded strongly of her father by this man, who was so powerfully indwelt by Jesus Christ.

In between the hymns he gave short, practical talks on Christian living. At one interval he said, 'I would like to know how many here have family prayers in their homes? All who do, hold up your hands.' The response evidently failed to satisfy him because he commented, 'That's far too few! How many of you will have family prayers from now on? Hands up!' Still the response wasn't good enough, so he once again encouraged the people to adopt the practice, so that the final count was bigger. Later on he asked, 'Who in this hall has read the Bible through from beginning to end?' Only about fifty hands were raised in the whole crowd. 'Ah! I've caught some of you preachers now!' he exclaimed, only half in jest. 'Not even you have read the whole Bible! Who will promise to read it right through in the coming twelve months? It can be done in that time, can't it, Dr Torrey?'

Torrey stood up. 'It most certainly can,' he agreed. 'Three chapters a day and five on Sundays will do it!'

Then there was more singing, and after that Dr Torrey mounted the dais and gave his sermon. It was a powerful, convincing gospel message and persuaded hundreds of people to commit their lives to Jesus Christ that night.

Straight after that first meeting Helen began to work among the women who had attended, listening to their problems and cares and pointing them towards Jesus as the answer. She was willing to talk to any sort of person, be they a wealthy lady or an impoverished factory girl in ragged clothes. She would share the gospel message with anyone who was willing to listen.

As she went home with her mother that evening she was brimming over with joy. It had been such a privilege to see God worshipped so heartily and to hear his gospel preached so powerfully that night, and then to have the opportunity of helping people to respond to it. Two of the women she had prayed with had received Christ as their Saviour and Lord. She was looking forward to the next four weeks. If the first night were as good as this, what would things be like later, when the campaign had reached fever pitch?

And there was something else that excited her that night – and that was Charles Alexander himself. What a wonderful man! She tried to suppress a girlish excitement which was bubbling up inside her, but it refused to go away. She could foresee that she was going to develop a full-blown crush on him.

Helen's mother was just as impressed by Alexander as her daughter was. A few days after the start of the campaign she invited him to spend his Sunday at 'Uffculme'. When Helen heard about this she became almost frenzied with excitement. She went to her bedroom and paced about for a long time, thinking the matter over. With a sort of embarrassed rapture she realised that she was in love with Charles Alexander. How absurd! She didn't even know him. How could she be in love with him? And yet she couldn't deny the strength of her feelings.

Why did she feel this way? Was it simply that she was allured by the glamour of this charismatic evangelist? But no – it was something more than that. There was a strange genuineness and sincerity about her feelings for him. Where had those feelings come from?. . .

But what hope could her love for him ever have? Why would a man like that – who had travelled the world in the cause of the gospel – ever notice her? With a stomach full of butterflies she got down on her knees beside her bed.

'Heavenly Father,' she prayed, 'you know my feelings towards this man. You know that I wish to be married and to serve you by being a good wife to a devout Christian man. If these feelings I have about Mr Alexander are merely foolishness, I pray that nothing will happen between him and me. But, if it is your perfect will for us to become husband and wife, please bring it about. I ask it in the name of the Lord Jesus. Amen.' She hardly knew how she had had the nerve to pray such a thing! And yet somehow it had felt right to pray that way.

Alexander duly came to 'Uffculme' that Sunday and proved to be a most charming guest. Whenever he spoke to Helen her heart raced. She fancied that there was a sort of searching and longing in his eyes when he looked at her, but she told herself that this impression was just a product of her over-excited imagination.

After Alexander had left Helen's mother remarked to her with a happy-yet-sad smile, 'Don't you think Mr Alexander resembles your father?'

Helen thought for a moment, and realised that she felt the same way. 'Yes, he is like Papa,' she agreed. 'He has the same unswerving loyalty to Christ, the same complete trust in the Bible.'

'Yes, and he has a big, sympathetic heart,' added her mother. 'He's very sensitive to others' feelings. I particularly noticed that.'

'He's very warm, cheerful and gracious too,' said Helen. 'What a lovely man!' she sighed.

Her mother regarded her with a knowing smile, and Helen blushed. 'You care for Mr Alexander, don't you, my dear?' she said, taking her daughter's hand in her own.

'Yes, Mama, I do,' replied Helen with another sigh. 'But would he ever care for me? Would he notice me?'

'I think he has already noticed you, my dear.'

'Really?' said Helen, nearly shrieking with excitement. 'Do you really think so?'

'Yes. There was something in his manner which told me he was attracted to you.'

That night Helen spent a long time on her knees. 'Oh, dear Lord,' she prayed, 'if it is your will, make us husband and wife – but only if it is your perfect will. I wish to do your will, not my own. I surrender all my feelings about Mr Alexander to you. And please reveal your will to him also. Thy will be done, Lord. Amen.'

****

During the four weeks of the mission at Bingley Hall a human tide daily surged in and out of the doors and the numbers swelled as the days went by. The last meeting of the campaign had a *grande finale* atmosphere to it, and it seemed that the crowds just didn't want to go home. Dr Torrey finished his sermon and quietly slipped away from the platform while one of his staff pronounced the Benediction. But then a great throng began to gather around the dais, trapping Alexander. Hundreds of hands stretched up to him, wanting to shake his, and there were many affectionate cries of farewell. He shook a number of hands and said goodbye to a few people, but quickly realised that the situation was fast getting out of hand and the meeting was about to degenerate into noisy disorder. He quickly asked his pianist, Robert Harkness, to play the melody of Isaac Watts' hymn, *When I Survey the Wondrous Cross*. The notes of the famous tune rang out across the auditorium.

'Friends,' cried Alexander, his powerful voice clearly audible above the hubbub, 'we must not close such a mission as we have had together like this. I appreciate your love, but I want our last vision to be of Jesus.' He sang two lines from the hymn's third verse:

> *See from his head, his hands, his feet,*
> *Sorrow and love flow mingled down.*

Straight away the crowd repeated the lines and then sang them again and again, each time more softly, more meditatively, as the impact of the words struck home. Finally they sang them in a whisper, with their heads bowed. When the people eventually lifted their eyes, they saw that Alexander had left the dais and slipped out of the hall. Now in a reverent, thoughtful mood, they quietly went to their homes.

Helen was deeply impressed by this. It was plain that there was not a shred of self-aggrandisement in Charles Alexander's character and that Jesus was the Lord of his life in every respect. As she went home she reflected that in this, as in so many other ways, he reminded her of her father.

Two days after the end of the Bingley Hall campaign Alexander was again being entertained at 'Uffculme'. He was his usual merry, friendly self, but he seemed to be agitated about something. Several times Helen noticed him gazing at her, and when she returned his gaze he would quickly turn away. Towards the end of the afternoon he approached her with a nervous yet eager expression on his face.

'It's really quite a fine afternoon, Miss Cadbury,' he said. 'Would it be all right if you and I took a stroll together in the garden?'

35

'Why, I'd be delighted to, Mr Alexander,' replied Helen, a slight tremor in her voice. 'I often walk in the grounds.'

And so they donned their overcoats and walked and chatted for a few minutes. After a while Alexander went quiet. Helen glanced at him. He seemed to be thinking deeply about something.

'Miss Cadbury . . .' he began, and then faltered. 'Miss Cadbury, there's something I would dearly like to discuss with you.'

Helen's heart began to beat faster. 'Really, Mr Alexander? Well – er – why don't we sit down, then?'

He nodded, and they sat upon a bench in the nearby summer house, looking out onto one of the garden's pools. It was surrounded by snowdrops emerging from the thin covering of snow that lay on the ground.

'Well, before I can say what I want to say, I feel I ought to tell you a little about myself,' he began. 'As you know, I've been working in evangelism for some years now, and I've found it immensely rewarding, and God's love and companionship has always been a great comfort to me. But to tell you the truth, I have always wanted to marry – I have always felt the need for a wife – for a companion with whom to share my life and work. I wanted a wife who loved Christ as much as I did and who cared as I did about winning souls to him. She had to be someone with a strong faith and a strong character – someone who could talk to anyone, rich or poor, and tell them about Jesus.

'Anyhow, over Christmas I was alone in my hotel room for a few days, suffering from a chill. I was very, very lonely – all I could think about was my desire to have a wife. I prayed about it a great deal, and left all my feelings and desires in the Lord's hands, trusting him to do what was best for me and for his kingdom – even if that meant a life of loneliness for me.

'Well, the mission here in Birmingham started up a short while after that, and I was still trusting God about the whole matter. Then, on the first night of the campaign, after the meeting had finished and the mission workers were talking with the people who had stayed behind for counselling, I noticed you, in conversation with some young girls.' He blushed and smiled bashfully. 'Well, Miss Cadbury, I was deeply impressed by you – by your sincerity, by your keenness to win souls to Christ, and by – and by your beauty. After that I began looking for you at the end of each meeting, and every night I saw you at work, telling people about Jesus.' He hesitated, fidgeting with his hands, unable to look her in the eye. Then he blurted out his confession: 'Well, to tell you the truth, Miss Cadbury, I began to wonder whether you might be the young lady the Lord had chosen to be my wife.'

He glanced at her for a moment and was encouraged to see that she did not seem offended but instead was excited and nervous, just as he was.

Helen's heart was pounding, and she felt as if her mouth had siezed up. But she managed to say: 'Do go on, Mr Alexander.'

'Miss Cadbury,' he continued, 'after spending Sunday with you and your mother the other week, my feelings for you grew stronger, and they're even stronger now. I've spent a lot of time praying to the Lord about this, Miss Cadbury – I want us to do his will, whatever that may be. But I feel it right that I should say – that is, that I should ask . . .' He fell silent for a moment, and then smiled shyly at her and said, 'Helen, I'm in love with you!'

She felt that she had completely lost the power of speech, but still managed to form some words: 'Why, Mr Alexander, I – I feel the same way about you!' she confessed, smiling and blushing girlishly.

Alexander's face erupted with joy. 'Really?' he said. 'Do – do you really?'

'I, too, want to marry,' she continued, 'but I have never met the right man. But – but you are a fine

Christian man, Mister Alexander, and I admire you deeply. I've been praying that the Lord would show us both his will.'

Neither of them could quite believe that this was really happening, and both felt at a loss for words. Finally he managed to say: 'Helen, do you – do you love me?'

'I do,' she said, almost whispering.

They both smiled, and then they laughed with relief and happiness.

'Can it really be true?' he said. 'Do you really feel about me the way I feel about you? Oh, praise God! This is no coincidence! Helen, I believe the Lord wants us to be together – how else could it be that we've been thinking the same things about each other?'

'I believe you're right,' agreed Helen. 'I think we both know the way the Lord is leading us, don't we?'

'I think we do!' agreed Charles with fervour. 'Oh, Helen, I care for you very much – I love you! Will you do me the honour of becoming my wife?'

Helen felt as if her whole body were trembling with a dizzy rapture. 'Yes, I will, Mr Alexander – Charles,' she said.

Silently, with a sort of reverence, Alexander took her hand and gently kissed it. Then he kissed her lightly on the lips.

Helen blushed deeply.

He offered her his arm. 'Shall we go back inside, Helen?' he asked with a big smile.

'Yes, let's – I can't wait to tell mother!'

4

Beginning the Great Adventure

Helen's mother was overjoyed by the exciting news which her daughter and Charles brought with them from the garden that afternoon in February, although she was a little taken aback by the suddenness of their decision. But she was swiftly reassured by their explanation of the matter and realised that they had been brought together by God. In the eyes of the world their engagement might seem hasty, but her eyes of faith could see the evidence of heaven's guidance. Emma felt that she could not wish or pray for a better husband for her daughter. Ever since Helen had lost her childhood faith she and her husband had prayed daily that she would return to Christ, and that prayer had been answered. Since then she had prayed that God would join Helen with a good Christian man who would strengthen her faith. Charles Alexander certainly fitted the bill. Another reason why Emma was so delighted by Helen's choice of husband was that Charles reminded her so much of her own Richard.

Straight away she invited Charles to stay at 'Uffculme' until the beginning of the forthcoming campaign in Dublin, even though he had planned to join Dr Torrey and the rest of the mission team for a holiday at Wynd Point, the Cadburys' beautiful country retreat in the Malvern Hills. They too were surprised but delighted by the news of Charles' engagement. Immediately Dr Torrey wrote to him:

I am glad of the news. I am sure you can do better work married, but I have never before met anyone whom I would have been glad to see you marry. Miss Cadbury will become more to you every year. You think you are in love now, but you won't know what love means until you have been married for years, as Mrs Torrey and I have.

After the announcement of their engagement letters congratulating Charles and Helen inundated 'Uffculme', coming from all over the British Isles. Lady Kinnaird, who with her husband had been among those closely involved in organising the Torrey-Alexander missions in Britain, wrote to Charles:

Lord Kinnaird and myself send you our best wishes for your happiness. Hers is a well-known and honoured name, and we pray God to bless you both. I am glad that this country, which owes you so much, gives you one of the best gifts, by God's guidance.

A Christian who had worked with Charles in Glasgow wrote to Helen about him:

A truer and more loving friend I do not know. He is so like his Master, and that smile upon his face has won many to the Saviour.

David Williamson, another supporter of the campaigns and a friend who had greatly helped Charles to understand the British approach to life, wrote to Helen:

Mr Alexander's friendship with me has been most intimate and happy. When I look at him, the phrase of Henry Drummond – 'one of Heaven's favourites' – comes to my mind. In all the days and in all the various experiences I have shared with him, there has been just the same crystal character exemplified. The life of an evangelist has its special trials, and yet it has been the noble task of many a wife to make her husband's work doubly effective. It means, for some, a perpetual giving-up, a yielding of home claims in order that God may be glorified in the sphere beyond the home. God gives his own letters of introduction, and I believe he has guided you two souls in this matter. Mr Alexander has had exhausting demands on his sympathies, and he will now have at least some return of the sympathy he has so freely given to the multitude.

The ten days between their engagement and Charles' departure for Ireland were some of the happiest in Helen's life. She and her fiance spent many hours together getting to know each other better. She had no doubts that she had made the right decision in agreeing to marry Charles, and grew to love him more with each passing day. The rapport between them was easy and natural and they felt that they could share everything with each other. They talked about their childhoods, their parents, their hopes for their future together, their faith. Charles was surprised to discover that Helen had some spiritual problems, and one day, while they were walking in the gardens, he asked her about them with his usual gentleness and tact.

'My parents were wonderful examples of real Christian faith,' explained Helen. 'So I always believed in God, and when I was twelve I gave my life to Jesus. Soon I started telling my schoolfriends about him, and quite a number were converted.'

'I might have guessed!' said Charles, his face glowing with admiration for his fiancee. 'I could tell from the very first time I set eyes on you that you had a passion for winning souls to Christ.'

'But I'm sorry to say that I turned away from the Lord at one time,' confessed Helen, her eyes downcast, ashamed to admit this to Charles.

He nodded in an understanding way. 'Tell me about it, my dear,' he said.

She was reassured by his loving attitude. She had half expected him to be piously shocked that she could ever have gone astray and had wondered if anyone with such a strong, radiant faith as his could possibly understand how a person could allow their love for Christ to grow cold.

'When I was at college in London I came under the influence of what they call the "higher criticism", since some of my tutors were of that persuasion,' she continued. 'And I'm afraid I was rather impressed by their views, and I began to despise the simple, straightforward faith I had had as a young girl. Gradually I began to lose sight of Jesus.'

'Yes, that's a very common story these days, Helen,' said Charles. 'In all the countries I've worked in, I've met a great many young people who have been influenced by rationalism and the higher criticism. So you're not alone, my dear.' He smiled at her encouragingly. 'I'm just so thankful that the Lord brought you back to himself again – thankful for your sake, and thankful for mine.' He took her hand and held it tenderly.

She turned and smiled at him. 'Dear Charles,' she said. 'I love you so very much.'

'I love you too, honey.'

It was the first time he had called her 'honey'. She loved the way he said it in his Southern accent.

'Tell me, how did the Lord win you back?' he asked as they continued walking.

'Through the death of my father,' she answered. 'My life was devastated by his passing away. I felt terribly lost without him, and in my grief I turned back to God. Gradually my old faith returned to me – but it was stronger than before. It was the faith of a woman rather than that of a child.'

'Well, if I needed further convincing that God had brought you and I together, what you've just said would convince me,' declared Charles, deeply moved. 'I think I had an experience very similar to yours. I gave my life to the Lord when I was a child, but when I became a young man I wanted to use my musical abilities to pursue a career on the stage. But then my daddy died, and through that the Lord called me away from my worldly ambitions and led me to work for him as an evangelist.'

'We have so much in common, don't we?' said Helen, touched by what Charles had told her.

They sat down upon one of the wooden benches in the grounds. 'Charles, it makes me sad to think of my college tutors, and all the other people in the world who think the same way as them,' said Helen. 'They're so blind, so lost. In a way they're more lost than heathens who have never so much as heard the name of Jesus. Those educated, cultured people have an opportunity to believe, but they love their own wisdom too much. They're so wise that they're foolish. They think they can reach God through the cleverness of their intellects. They are proud – they are too proud of their knowledge to admit that they are sinners just as much as the most ignorant of people, and that they need Christ to save them from their sins just as much as the uneducated do.'

'Perhaps people like your tutors have never really heard the true gospel preached,' reflected Charles. 'They think they know what the Christian faith is all about, but really they don't. No-one has ever told them in plain, unmistakable terms that they're sinners and that unless they recieve Jesus as their Saviour they will go to hell when they die. Dr Torrey and I make a point of never beating about the bush in our campaigns – we feel it's our solemn duty to tell the people the truth. Of course, we tell them about God's infinite love too, and we tell them that he will forgive and save anyone who truly repents, but we make sure they understand what will happen to them if they don't put their faith in Jesus.'

Helen was silent, and looked troubled. 'Charles, you believe that everything in the Bible is true, don't you? Literally true, I mean.'

'Well, yes, I do, my dear,' he replied. 'Do you have difficulty believing all that the Bible says?'

'I'm afraid I do. Can one really take all of it literally? Of course I believe the central truths of the gospel which the Bible teaches, and I'm sure the New Testament must be reliable history, but can one accept all of the Old Testament at face value? For example, can we really believe that the Red Sea parted so that the children of Israel could pass through it?'

'Honey, I think you have to ask yourself a question,' said Charles gently. 'Is the Bible the authoritative Word of God or not? Is it true or is it not true? If it is, one must believe all of it. If it isn't, then it must just be a collection of myth and folklore and dubious history. No middle ground is possible. One can't say that perhaps the Bible is true 'in a sense', because how does one decide in what sense? And one can't say that perhaps some parts of it are literally true and others aren't, because then one has to decide which parts, and how does one do that? Deciding in which sense we should believe the Bible or which parts of it we should believe becomes a matter of mere personal preference.

'And I don't think one can say that the New Testament is reliable history while saying that the Old Testament isn't. Why should the New Testament necessarily be more reliable than the Old? If the miracles in the Old Testament aren't true, then why are the ones in the New? If we say the power of God didn't really part the Red Sea, how can we say that same power really raised Jesus from the dead? I think one either has to believe all of the Bible or none of it. I think that's what you need to decide in your heart of hearts, honey. Really you need to choose between belief and unbelief. Will you believe God's Word or won't you?'

Helen was impressed by Charles' arguments, and once again recognised in him a strong faith like that of her father. 'I will have to think about all these things, Charles,' she said.

He was quiet for a moment, considering what he had just said. 'Helen, I've not been harsh with you, have I?' He asked with concern.

She smiled at him. 'No – no, not at all. But you've given me a great deal to ponder.'

'Yes, I know I have, honey. But will you promise me one thing?'

'Yes. What?'

'Will you promise me you'll ask the Lord to show you the truth about his Word? Will you ask him to answer all your questions and doubts for you?'

'Yes. I promise that I will.'

'Good. He'll do it for you. I know he will!'

They had many other conversations like this in those last two weeks of February, and Helen felt that her mind was just as disturbed by Charles as her heart was full of love for him.

All too soon the time came when Charles had to go to Ireland. It was a sad parting, since they knew that they would see very little of each other for months to come, as the Dublin campaign was just one of a whole series of forthcoming Torrey-Alexander missions in the British Isles. They would be apart most of the time until July, when their wedding would take place. The two lovers promised to pray for and write to each other every day. While travelling to Dublin Charles wrote to Helen:

My dear 'Answer to Prayer', you seem to almost have a halo about you, as I think of you as an answer from on high to my call. God will keep this new union of ours, and I feel sure His Spirit led you to quote the verse: 'Perfect love casteth out fear.' It seems almost too much to believe that you can really love one whom you have known so short a time.

45

The Dublin campaign lasted throughout March. While Charles was there congratulations started to arrive at 'Uffculme' from his homeland, the USA. The Leavitt family in Waterloo, Iowa, with whom Charles had lived for six years, were overjoyed by the news of his engagement. Lucy Leavitt wrote to Charles:

It seems too good to be true, but no better than you deserve. You have succeeded in making so many people happy that it is only fair that you should now have your full share. Father was so interested he wanted to start for England at once to see the bride-elect!

Another of Charles' American friends, William A. Sunday, wrote to Helen:

You already have thousands of friends over here, for every one who is a friend of Charles is also a friend of yours. I know you must be a sensible, kind-hearted, and most estimable young lady, or Charles would never have asked you to become Mrs Alexander, and I congratulate you on having exercised such admirable judgement, for you have secured one of our very best. Charles and I are old friends and have fought many a battle for Christ and truth.

For Helen the high point of every day of their separation was writing to her beloved Charles and receiving his letters. Their love deepened as they got to know each other more intimately by setting down their thoughts and feelings on paper. On March 4th Charles wrote:

I sit here and recall your sweet face as you chatted on hour after hour in your sane, wholesome, honest, sweet way. I have locked you up in a room I had despaired of ever having filled – the banquet room of my heart.

In another letter he said:

My 'Loved and Longed-for,' my heart seems as if it would melt sometimes whenever a suggestion of you comes to my mind. Only a few short weeks, and yet I feel as if I had always known you, and you were made for me.

In another:

There was a dignity and warmth about your letter this morning that left such a steady glow upon my soul, that the whole day has been sweetened, and a number of people have received kind words because of it. I consider letter-writing a God-given method of doing good.

Helen wrote to him:

My dearest Charles, it is difficult for me to find the words to convey how much I miss you, now that you are away in Ireland. And yet I would not have you here with me, because if you were you would not be serving our Lord as you should, and in no way would I ever want to distract you from your work for Him. Rather, I hope and pray that as husband and wife we will serve Him together, each helping the service of the other. I am so glad that the work in Dublin is going so well – my heart fills with a wifely pride to think that the man I love should be so greatly used by the Lord to win souls to Christ. I miss you so much, my dearest, even though I have known you such a short time. Uffculme now seems a quiet, empty place without the sound of your conversation and your happy laughter, and the rooms seem dull and drab without your bright, cheerful smile.

During the months of their separation Helen was far from idle, since she spent her time writing a biography of her beloved late father. She also did some hard thinking about her faith and, helped by the encouragement and gentle challenge in Charles' letters and by the Christian books which he sent with them, she gradually came to the conclusion that he was right about the authority of the Bible, and that all of it should be accepted as the Word of God. She was deeply relieved that this difference of opinion between them had been resolved and that she was now fully satisfied about the matter in her own mind. She felt that there was now nothing which could hamper them in serving the Lord together as husband and wife.

In April the Torrey-Alexander team came back to England to lead a mission in Bristol, moving on to Bradford in May and finally Brighton in June. It was there that Helen's younger sister Margaret, having been challenged earlier by conversations she had had with Charles, definitely accepted Jesus as her Saviour. During these busy months Charles and Helen only occasionally had the chance to spend a few precious hours together, when either Helen would visit Charles at his work or he would go to 'Uffculme' for a short rest. Everywhere they went Charles' and Dr Torrey's efforts were rewarded with great success. Vast numbers of people became Christians and all over the country the Church was strengthened and inspired by their influence and example.

Then, finally, at the end of June Charles' engagements came to an end, and he was able to rejoin his fiancee in Birmingham. He stepped through the doorway of 'Uffculme' and received a hearty welcome from Helen and her family. She and Charles spent the next two weeks being alone together as much as possible and making plans for their married life. These included building a new home for themselves on a piece of land just a stone's throw from 'Uffculme'.

Finally the day they had so long awaited arrived – Thursday 14th July, 1904. It was a bright and sunny day and the gardens of 'Uffculme' were ablaze with flowers of every hue and fragrance. After a hectic morning of preparation, Helen was finally ready. Looking magnificent in her flowing, white dress, she got into the carriage which awaited her, accompanied by her mother, her eldest brother Barrow, her sister Margaret and Dr Torrey's daughter Blanche, the latter two dressed as bridesmaids. The other six bridesmaid – her sister Beatrice and five of her young nieces and cousins – got into a second carriage.

Helen had expected to be very nervous, and it was true that her heart was pounding, but her joy overshadowed all other feelings. Finally the carriages arrived at the Friends' Meeting House in Bull Street in the city, where a large crowd of wellwishers had gathered to see the bride. They cheered as she got down from the carriage, assisted by the driver. It was just after one o'clock – perfect timing. The bride would be just a little late, as tradition demanded. Charles, who had stayed the previous night and this morning at the home of a friend, would be waiting inside.

Helen's mother kissed her, her eyes tearful.

'Don't be nervous, my dear,' she said. 'This is your great day – enjoy it!'

Then Barrow led her by the arm into the meeting house, while Helen waited outside with her throng of bridesmaids. A few moments later he returned, smiling.

'Are you ready, little sister?' he asked.

'Yes, I think so,' replied Helen.

'Then let's go in!' Barrow offered her his arm and they entered together. There was murmur of delight among the hundreds of guests who had been invited to the wedding as they caught sight of the bride at the door.

49

They had come from all over the British Isles, and quite a number of Charles' friends and relatives from America were present. However, sadly circumstances had prevented any of his immediate family from attending. In accordance with Quaker custom, there were no flowers adorning the meeting house, but the joyful purpose of the occasion was better than any mere decoration. In the centre of the room stood Charles – tall, dignified and very smart. His face lit up when he saw Helen enter. Beside him stood the even taller figure of Arthur Bradley, his colleague and best man.

A breathless hush descended upon the meeting as Barrow led the bride up the aisle. The bridesmaids followed them two by two, all clad in shimmering white and carrying graceful, simple bouquets of yellow marguerites. The first pair were Margaret and Blanche, behind them were Beatrice and the five little nieces and cousins.

Helen had eyes only for her husband-to-be, gazing upon him lovingly through her soft bridal veil as she came up the aisle, feeling as if she were walking on air. Then she was beside him, and he gave her a smile full of joy and pride. A crescent of empty seats faced the guests, and the whole bridal party now sat down upon them. Helen was seated between her mother and her fiance.

Since so many of the people present were not familiar with the customs of the Society of Friends, one of the elders of the fellowship stood and said a few words explaining the Quaker way of conducting a wedding. The ceremony was to be very simple and, as with all Quaker meetings, without any formal order of service. This introduction was followed by a few moments of silent prayer, and then Helen's uncle George stood and prayed aloud:

'Dear Heavenly Father, we ask thee this day to bless this man and this woman as they declare before thee and before this congregation their vows of matrimony.

We ask thee to bless their union, that they may love, help, encourage and care for each other. We ask thee to bless their marriage with children and to strengthen them as they endeavour to raise godly offspring. We pray these prayers in the blessed name of our Saviour, the Lord Jesus Christ. Amen.'

Then there was another time of silent prayer. After a while Charles turned to Helen and whispered, 'Shall we stand up now?' Together they rose from their seats, and the bridesmaids did likewise. Helen thought with amusement that it must have looked to the guests like the rising of a foam-crested wave. Then Charles took Helen's right hand in his own and said these words:

'Friends, in the fear of the Lord, and in the presence of this assembly, I take this my friend, Helen Cadbury, to be my wife, promising through divine assistance to be unto her a loving and faithful husband, until it shall please the Lord by death to separate us.' His fine voice had rung out clearly in the crowded room, although because of the importance of the occasion it had sounded a little more tremulous than it did when it was used to address thousands of people in a mission meeting. Then Helen, in a slightly faltering voice, made a similar declaration:

'Friends, in the fear of the Lord, and in the presence of this assembly, I take this my friend, Charles Alexander, to be my husband, promising through divine assistance to be unto him a loving and faithful wife, until it shall please the Lord by death to separate us.'

They took their seats once again, and with trembling hands Charles gently slipped a golden ring upon Helen's finger. There then followed further periods of silent prayer, interspersed by short spoken prayers and words of encouragement and advice to the couple from Dr Torrey and other people in the congregation. Then there were some beautiful readings from Scripture on the theme of Christian marriage. Finally the marriage certificate was signed by Charles, Helen and their four witnesses, Helen's mother and brother and Dr and Mrs Torrey.

And so the wedding was over. Charles and Helen calmly walked back down the aisle, watched by the smiling guests. Then there was a drive through Birmingham's crowded streets back to 'Uffculme'. The reception was held in the spacious grounds, where the bridal pair stood beneath a large marquee and greeted the hundreds of friends who had come to share in their happiness.

Finally, when all the formalities of the day were finished, it was time for the newly-weds to depart for Wynd Point, where they were to spend their wedding night. With tears of happiness Helen said goodbye to her family and got into a carriage with Charles. Together they set off for the Malvern Hills, beginning the great adventure that was married life.

5

A Busy Honeymoon

Helen and Charles stood together on the deck of the S.S. *Lucania* in the early morning of 23rd July as she drew near to New York harbour. It was a fine, sunny day, although a little windy out on the open water. They had had a wonderful time together since their wedding. They had spent a day at Wynd Point, strolling in the beautiful countryside, enjoying just being alone together after all the hubbub of the previous day. Then on the Saturday morning they had caught the train to Liverpool and had later boarded the *Lucania*. The voyage had lasted for a week and had been a blissful time for them both. It seemed such a luxury to be together so much, since they had been separated throughout most of their engagement.

The ship steamed up New York harbour, passed the Statue of Liberty and threaded its way among the ferry boats and other ships which plied the waters. The couple disembarked from the ship full of almost childish excitement, about to begin a busy six-week-long tour of the States. Charles felt proud to be introducing his beloved bride to his home country, while she was keen to see as much as possible of the native land of the man she loved.

They spent all of that first day seeing the sights of Manhattan and calling upon some of Charles' friends, staying the night in the Netherland Hotel on Fifth Avenue, at the corner of Central Park. The next day they went on to Philadelphia, where Helen introduced her husband to some of her American relatives, whose ancestors had emigrated to the USA in the last century. The couple spent a beautiful summer's day sailing up the mighty Hudson River from New York in a steamboat. They visited the city of Albany, where Charles took Helen for a ride in an American Buggy, a light two-wheeled vehicle drawn by a single horse. They toured New England, passing through little towns of neat, white-painted frame houses. Helen thought the countryside looked like parkland, since there were no fences or hedges marking the divisions between the properties.

After seeing the magnificent Niagara Falls, they moved on to the great, bustling city of Chicago, where a big reception had been arranged for them at the Moody Bible Institute, the college founded by the world-famous evangelist, Dwight L Moody. Charles had studied there when younger and had very fond memories of the place. After they had stopped off for a few days at the enormous World's Fair at St Louis, Missouri, and on 16th August they reached Knoxville, Tennessee, Charles' home town. His mother, sister and brothers gave them a royal welcome. Charles took great delight in showing his wife around the haunts of his boyhood. Everywhere his old friends greeted him as if he were a long-lost brother, and they were all keen to meet his English bride, whom they loved straight away for his sake. He even took her to the sweet shop he had often visited as a youth and bought her five cents' worth of the cinnamon drops he had used to buy himself!

It was very hard for the couple to tear themselves away from the family at Knoxville, but the parting was made easier for them by the fact that Charles' brother Homer was able to come to England with them, and by the knowledge that the rest of the family would come and visit them there in the near future. So Charles, Helen and Homer sped back across the country to New York and sailed for England abroad the S.S. *Oceanic*, after a very busy but highly enjoyable honeymoon.

After arriving at Liverpool they went straight home to 'Uffculme' and were warmly welcomed by Helen's mother and sisters. But they could only spend two days there before leaving again, since Charles and his partner Dr Torrey now had to begin a series of campaigns which would take up all their time for many months ahead. Charles, Helen, Dr Torrey and the mission team spent September in Bolton in Lancashire, holding evangelistic meetings in a large hall. Most of those who attended were poor cotton mill workers, and great numbers of them received Christ as their Saviour.

In October the team went to Cardiff. The Welsh people, traditionally ardent singers, quickly took to the new revival melodies taught to them by Charles Alexander. The month-long campaign in Wales was probably one of the factors which contributed to the great spiritual revival which was to sweep through the whole Principality shortly afterwards.

One of the most memorable events in the early part of Charles' and Helen's marriage occurred during the great campaign which was held at Liverpool from November 1904 to the end of January 1905. More than a year had gone by since the first Torrey-Alexander mission in the city, held in the Philharmonic Hall. Since that time the Tournament Hall, a great building of glass and iron, had been constructed near Edge Lane, one of the city's sub-urbs. In spite of heavy snow the first meeting in the hall, which could seat twelve thousand five hundred people, was packed out. The choir which had been formed for the campaign was the largest one ever assembled for such an evangelistic endeavour and numbered over three thousand six hundred.

The people who had been members of the choir of the previous campaign, who now made up a large part of the new choir, had great affection for Charles Alexander, who had made so deep an impression upon them and their city, so they wanted to offer some kind of wedding gift to him and his bride. However, it was felt that any lavish material gift would be inappropriate, since poverty was rife in Liverpool that winter. So it was decided instead to give a great 'wedding feast' to the poor of the city in honour of the Alexanders. It was held on 7th January, 1905, and was a remarkable occasion. The central area of the hall was filled with trestle tables loaded with good food and brightly decorated with vases of flowers. About half of the great choir was seated upon the platform at the front of the hall, while the other half stood ready to wait upon the guests. In the galleries of the hall were thousands of onlookers who had come to enjoy the evening. Two thousand three hundred guests from the poorest areas of the city came to the feast. When they entered the hall their faces were sad and downcast, but as the great meal progressed and they enjoyed the food and drink, they became more cheerful. Finally the tables were cleared and the vases were taken away. Many of the guests put the flowers in their worn buttonholes or pinned them to their faded shawls.

Then Dr J. Louis Fenn, one of the chief organisers of the campaign, went up on to the red-carpeted dais at the front of the hall and said a few words:

'I am sure the members of the choir and many other folk here tonight do not need me to remind them of the great mission which Dr Torrey and Mr Alexander led here in our city of Liverpool last year. The memory of it is still fresh in our minds and hearts. We remember how God blessed us so richly through their work – God blessed our own individual lives, the lives of our churches, and the life of our whole city!' There was a great burst of spontaneous applause.

'We hold both these two gentlemen in very high regard, and so we were all thrilled when we learned just a few months ago that Mr Alexander was engaged to be married to the daughter of the late Richard Cadbury, of Birmingham, that great Christian man who in his lifetime did so much to help the poor and needy. How proud we were to know that Mr Alexander, one of

America's finest men, was to be wed to a young lady from such an outstanding Christian English family! And tonight our joy and happiness is all the greater, because we have been celebrating their marriage by holding this wedding feast. Mr Alexander, will you come and say a few words, please?' There was another surge of applause as Charles mounted the steps of the dais.

'My friends,' he said, addressing the vast choir, his face radiating happiness and gratitude, 'I want to thank you from the bottom of my heart for this beautiful wedding gift which you have given my wife and I. Nothing else you could have given us could have delighted us more, and nothing else could have been a better expression of true Christian charity.

'Well, I'm sure you want to know a little bit about how Mrs Alexander and I met and became man and wife. The long and the short of it is, it was the Lord who made our marriage. For a long time we had both prayed for him to give us the right marital partner, so that we could serve him better. While I was at the mission in Birmingham last year he drew the two of us together and it wasn't long before we knew that the Lord, in his love and wisdom, had graciously answered our prayers and had chosen us as husband and wife for each other.

'But now I want you to meet my dear wife!' he said, smiling happily. He beckoned to Helen, who had been sitting at the foot of the dais, and led her up the steps. The great crowd now burst into thunderous applause. Thousands of handkerchiefs were swiftly produced from the pockets of the choir members and were waved in affectionate greeting. It was an extraordinary sight – it looked as if a huge cloud of fluttering white butterflies had entered the hall. Helen was nervous about making a public appearance before so many people, but she was reassured by the warmth of their feeling towards her. These people loved her because they loved Charles. It was one of the most moving moments of her life.

At a gesture from Charles the great crowd fell silent. Helen had a fine voice for public speaking and now, despite being deeply moved by the occasion, confidently said these few words: 'I am very grateful to you all for your warm and loving welcome, and for the wonderful gift which you have given my husband and I. Thank you all so much.' Her eyes were misting over with emotion. 'Please pray for us as we seek to serve the Lord Jesus together.' As she finished speaking there was more heartfelt applause.

Then Dr Torrey gave one of his earnest, compelling gospel addresses, and appealed to those in the crowd who wanted to commit their lives to Christ to make a decision that night. Two hundred and seventeen people from all over the hall responded to his call. It was a night which Charles and Helen would cherish in their hearts for the rest of their lives.

From the beginning of February 1905 to early July the Torrey-Alexander team ran a huge campaign in London. Although they had held a three-week-long mission at Mildmay in 1903, they had as yet made no attempt to reach the whole city with the gospel. Working with the London churches, this was the task which they now undertook. The Royal Albert Hall was booked for the whole of February and March. A large temporary wooden building was to be erected in Brixton so that the campaign could reach the southern half of the great metropolis in April and May, and the Salvation Army's huge corrugated-iron prefabricated building, used in previous Torrey-Alexander missions, was to be set up on the Aldwych site in the Strand so that the campaign could continue throughout June.

Charles and Helen needed lodgings for the duration of the campaign, so they rented a small furnished house in Gloucester Road, about twenty minutes' walk from the Albert Hall. This was the nearest thing to a marital home they had so far known, since the house they were building near 'Uffculme' was not yet completed. Here

58

they spent together the few precious hours of leisure time they had while in London.

The interest aroused in the campaign by widespread publicity and by the united prayers of the London churches was so great that over forty thousand applications for tickets to the first Albert Hall meeting were received. The organisers were inundated with requests for membership of the choir, but these had to be rejected once its numbers had reached four thousand.

The opening meeting of the campaign, on 4th February, was a memorable occasion. The Albert Hall was packed out, and thousands of people who had been unable to gain admission waited in the streets outside. Charles had been suffering from a heavy cold and had only just left his sick bed earlier that day, but the organisers of the campaign had been praying earnestly that he would be able to perform to the best of his ability. When the time came for the meeting to start he went onto the platform, his figure radiating a confidence that God would work through him that night. There was an enthusiastic round of welcoming applause. For a few moments he stood impassively, casting his gaze over the great sea of faces as a hubbub of anticipation rippled through it. He prayed a silent prayer for wisdom and guidance. Then his pianist, Robert Harkness, struck up the opening notes of that famous hymn, *Abide with me*. Harkness continued playing softly as Charles prayed out loud:

'Heavenly Father, we wish to dedicate this campaign to you this evening. We ask you to work mightily in the city of London over the coming months; we ask you to touch many hearts by the preaching of your Word by Dr Torrey; we ask you to save many souls through the songs we will be learning and singing – we ask that those songs will be sung throughout London and that they will bring thousands into your Kingdom.'

Then he announced the first hymn, *Oh, it is wonderful*, and the crowds sang it with gusto. His face lit up with pleasure at their hearty response. The words of the hymn rolled in great waves of sound through the hall. The volume diminished as the people sang the tender words:

> Oh, it is wonderful,
> That He should care for me
> Enough to die for me!
> Oh, it is wonderful, wonderful, to me!

The opening meeting was a promising start to the campaign and as the weeks and months went by the lives of countless people in the great capital of the British Empire were changed by the powerful ministry of Torrey and Alexander. Time and again in the years to come in many different parts of the world Charles and Helen were to meet people who had been blessed by the London mission and were to come across many who had found Christ through it. People came to the meetings not only from London but also from all over the British Isles and from many other lands. One evening Charles asked people in the auditorium to stand up when he called out the name of their native land. He found that in the audience there were visitors from America, Australia, France, Germany, Russia, Switzerland, Scandinavia and even far-away Japan.

The London mission made a great impression not only in church circles but also among the secular press and professional musicians. The eminent music critic, H. Hamilton Fyfe, attended the opening meeting on 4th February and in the *Daily Mirror* described Charles as:

the most remarkable conductor I have ever seen. I have watched the methods and the triumphs of the most famous baton-wielders of the time – Colonne, Nikisch, Mottl, Weingartner, and Henry J. Wood. Never have I been so much impressed as I was by this bright-faced, energetic young evangelist. As the leader of a choir he has an amazing and almost magical influence, not only over the trained choir; he simply makes everybody sing, and sing as he wants them to. 'Watch my hand!' he calls, and the men's unaccompanied voices rise and fall in crooning cadences with an effect any conductor might be proud of. Watch his hands? Why, we are watching every part of him; we cannot take our eyes off him; we are fascinated, hypnotized, bewitched. Never for a moment is he still. Now we see him 'fine down' a passage from *fortissimo* to *piano*. All done by a turn of the wrist! That marvellous magic hand of his thrills with the feeling he wants to put into the music. 'Sing it as if you meant it!' he cries to the choir. But they do mean it. This is no pretence; no artistic make-believe. That is why the singing is unlike anything I have ever heard before. That – and the wonderful conducting of this astonishing young man.

Another famous journalist, James Douglas, wrote in the *Morning Leader*:

Alexander is more than a choir conductor. He is a crowd conductor. In ten minutes he turns this huge multitude into a choir. He teaches them to obey him. He gives them singing lessons. That superb hymn, *Abide with Me*, serves as an example of his method. He first makes his choir whisper it, sigh it, croon it, murmur it. Then he calls on the crowd. 'Don't look at your books; look at me!' and the crowd follows the flowing gestures. . .The climax is the *Glory Song*, the battle hymn of the Revival. 'I want you to sing it all the rest of your life. It will do you good!' The choir sings it. The tune is catching, and the crowd swiftly snatches it. 'You've been practising!' The crowd laughs like a happy child.

Friends will be there I have loved long ago.

This is the first line of the last stanza. He calls upon those who have lost loved ones to sing it. As the crowd sings there is a tragic wail in the music. But the master-stroke is a hymn with the heart-rending refrain, *Tell mother I'll be there*, based upon President McKinley's telegram to his dying mother. As Alexander sings the chorus in clear, poignant, staccato tones, the hall is hushed with emotion. . .The dynamite of the revival is Alexander the Great – he will make London hum, for he will make London sing.

Charles believed that God was infinitely worthy of worship, and so worship was to him an immensely important human activity in its own right. However, there was also a pragmatic side to his passion for praise. He sincerely believed that people would go to hell if they did not receive Jesus Christ as their personal Saviour and Lord. He was appalled by the thought that there were untold millions of people in the world who were heading for a Christless eternity after death, and so that same thought motivated him to carry out a vigorous evangelistic ministry. Early in his life he had discovered the power of praise. He had found that whenever God was truly worshipped, then he would work mightily in people's lives. And so it was that Charles used gospel hymns and songs to bring those who did not know Christ to faith in him.

Many of those who came to the Torrey-Alexander meetings were completely unchurched and had previously had no interest in Christianity whatsoever because it had been so poorly presented to them in the past. However, at the meetings they truly experienced the reality of God, perhaps for the first time in their lives. Through the beautiful music and singing, through the powerful words of the songs, through the radiant faith of Charles Alexander, through the compelling preaching of Dr Torrey, their hearts and minds would be touched by God – they would be convicted of their sins and encouraged by the discovery that God loved them and was willing to forgive them and receive them as his children. Great numbers of them made professions of faith in Christ at the meetings, while many others gave themselves to him in the days and weeks that followed, as they thought over the things they had heard and as the gospel songs they had learned remained in their hearts and on their lips.

Charles' and Dr Torrey's ministry was also aimed at those who were already Christians. Through an experience of true worship and through hearing the Word of God faithfully preached during their missions, great numbers of churchgoers were brought into a renewed and deepened love for Christ and were challenged to serve him with greater zeal.

****

The great London mission was over, and Charles and Helen had briefly returned to Birmingham, because the building of their permanent marital home was now finished. They stood together on the lawn facing the front of the house, gazing upon it with a sort of childlike wonder.

'Is it really ours, Charles?' asked Helen. 'Is it really our home?'

Charles grinned. 'It's a wonderful gift from the Lord, isn't it?' he said.

'We'll have to give it a name, won't we?' said Helen. 'A big house like this can't be without a name. What shall we call it?'

Charles' face lit up. 'I've had an idea!' he announced. 'Can we call it 'Tennessee', after my home state? Sometimes I really miss the place, you know. If we gave the house that name, it would be like a little piece of Tennessee, right here in England.'

'That's a wonderful idea, Charles!' said Helen with enthusiasm.

'You're sure you don't mind? You're sure you like the name?'

'I love the name!' she exclaimed, and to prove it she walked up to the large front door, spread her arms wide and said in a loud voice, 'House, I name thee "Tennessee"!' Then she turned to Charles and laughed girlishly.

Charles laughed too and went and kissed her. 'I love you, honey,' he said.

They entered the house and spent their first night in it. However, it was also to be their last for quite some time, because on the following day they had to set off for America, where Charles and Dr Torrey were to take part in a number of missions. The Alexanders left their new home in the care of a housekeeper.

At Liverpool they boarded the S.S. *Carpathia* with Helen's mother and sister Beatrice, who were making their first visit to North America. On reaching the States Charles proudly showed them many of the sights, just as he had done for Helen. They all attended the Christian Workers' Conference at Northfield, Massachussetts, where Charles led a series of worship meetings.

It was while they were at Northfield that Helen first started suffering from sharp abdominal pains. A doctor diagnosed the trouble as appendicitis, but since the pains eased off after a few days he decided there was no need for surgery. At that time operations were dangerous and were usually carried out only as a last resort.

Charles still had a number of engagements to fulfil in America, so he and Helen had to part for a few weeks so that she and her mother could prepare 'Tennessee' for a visit by Charles' mother, his sister Ida and his brother Leo in August. This parting was difficult for them both. Just before Helen boarded the steamer bound for England Charles kissed his wife tenderly and pressed a note in an envelope into her hand. 'Please read this once you've set sail, honey,' he said. He stood on the dock and waved to them as the ship moved off down New York harbour. When Charles was no longer visible even as a dot in the far distance Helen went to her cabin and opened the envelope. It read:

I am more convinced than ever that you are the greatest woman I have ever known, or will know; and that I love you more deeply, I need not say, for you have seen it in my eyes. Good-bye, honey, my soul is filled with singing. We have reason to thank God that we have had a safe journey thus far. Anything you do for my mother, Ida, and Leo, will draw the golden cords tighter.

Helen wept with happiness that her husband loved her so much.

Charles' family arrived in Birmingham shortly after Helen's, and the two tribes had a convivial time together. To top it all, Charles himself arrived at 'Tennessee' about ten days later, to everyone's delight. However, he could only stay for two days, because he had to begin work for the forthcoming mission in Sheffield. Early in October Charles' family sailed home, having forged permanent friendships with the Cadburys. At this time Helen also had to say farewell to her sister Margaret. Back in the summer she had married Dr Neville Bradley, a Liverpool clergyman whom she had met a year earlier at Helen and Charles' wedding, and now the two of them were going to South China to take charge of a large Church Missionary Society hospital.

Charles and Helen were separated for much of the time over the coming months, since after the Sheffield mission there was a campaign in Plymouth in October and another in Oxford in November. Helen went to see her husband during these missions as often as she could and helped with the personal counselling of people who wanted to commit their lives to Christ, since soul-winning was as much of a passion with her now as it had been in her school days. However, the abdominal pains which had started in America kept recurring, so she had to spend much of her time resting at home. While they were apart she and Charles wrote to each other daily. While he was at Oxford she wrote to him:

> My dearest Charles, words cannot express how much I miss you, and how I long to be with you. I am so sorry, my dearest, that I cannot be with you – I do so want to support you and encourage you in your work for the Lord. I would give anything to be able to be with you at the end of a hard day's labour.

Charles replied:

> I am sure I have never loved you as I do now, you brave, sweet, lonely girl. I am sure the Lord will reward you for allowing me to stay here and work for him when you need me so much. Dr Torrey has been most tender to me, and said he was led out in prayer for you. I feel confident that God is answering our prayers, and is revealing himself clearly and giving you peace.

After the end of the Oxford mission a great farewell meeting for the Torrey-Alexander team was held at the Tournament Hall in Liverpool to mark the end to the great three-year-long series of campaigns which they had conducted in the British Isles. Then Torrey and his family sailed for America, leaving Charles to follow them a few weeks later. Just as Great Britain had been stirred by the news of the Torrey-Alexander campaigns in Australia and New Zealand, so now the United States and Canada were buzzing with reports of what God had been doing through these remarkable evangelists in the British Isles, and a whole series of missions in North America had been planned. The first was to be in Toronto at the end of December 1905, followed by others in Ottawa, Philadelphia and Atlanta.

However, it was becoming increasingly clear that Helen would not be able to accompany her husband to North America, since her abdominal problem showed no signs of disappearing, and the strain of travel would very probably exacerbate it. The pain of their parting was terrible, because they knew they would not see each other at all for several months and they were both deeply concerned about Helen's continuing illness. But although they parted with tears and pain, they also parted with hearts full of trust in God. On the train to Liverpool, from where Charles would set sail to America, he wrote:

> My heart and thoughts are with you. Thank our Beatrice for her intelligent, loving sympathy. I am sure mother is doing all she can to make it easier for you. Most of all, I know where permanent help and peace come from. I am depending on Him. Nothing rested me more today than when you said He was giving you peace more than you thought possible.

Charles' anxieties about Helen increased as the news about her health which he received from England got progressively worse, and their hopes that she would be able to join him in America in the Spring of 1906 were disappointed. In May he wrote to her:

> I think if you were here I could hardly bear you out of my sight. Each day, as my work is finished, I feel that I have worked for God, and my lovely Helen. How I had looked forward to showing you the people and places of the South. . .You are still my Gibraltar. If I did not have such confidence in the unshakeableness

67

of your love, there would be nothing strong enough to keep me here.

This experience of prolonged illness was a great trial to Helen, as she was an energetic woman in both body and mind and hated having to be idle. But the pain she was suffering was sometimes so acute that she could do nothing but stay in bed. Sometimes depression threatened to overwhelm her and she wondered anxiously whether the illness would claim her life. However, her faith in God was a great help to her. She knew in her heart that no sickness could be fatal if it were her Lord's will that she should still serve him on earth. Writing letters to her beloved husband and receiving letters from him was another great encouragement to her. However, because she did not wish to worry him needlessly, she concealed from him the true seriousness of her condition and did not let him know that she was often bedridden. In June she wrote to him:

My dear, dear Charles, I love you so much. I miss you more than I can possibly say. But although I cannot be with you in body, through my prayers I am with you in spirit. Constantly I ask our dear Father to strengthen you and to draw especially close to you, since I cannot comfort you with my own presence. So when you receive special blessing from the Lord, remember that it will be partly through my prayers. And so, by the grace of God, I will be with you in a sense. Do not fret about me, my love – I am in the most capable and loving of Hands.

In June the North American missions came to a close. The Torrey-Alexander team had made a huge impression everywhere they went, and during the campaigns no fewer than fifteen thousand people had made public professions of faith in Christ. Unknown to Torrey or Alexander at the time, the conclusion of these missions also marked the end of their working relationship, which had lasted since early in 1902, since God was afterwards to lead them in separate directions.

Charles, now free to return to England in July, wrote to Helen:

> Oh, honey, you don't know how hungry I am to feel the touch of your dear hand, and to look into your wonderful eyes. I need not say how my heart aches for my darling, with all of her suffering. . . My heart leaps when I think of seeing you.

A few days later he set sail from Montreal and early in July arrived at 'Tennessee'. As he entered Helen's room he rushed to her bedside without a word and took her in his arms. Neither of them spoke for some moments, but finally Helen, weeping with relief, managed to say, 'Oh, Charles . . .I've missed you so much. . .'

'I've missed you too, honey – more than I can ever say,' he replied, his voice choked emotion.

They were silent for a while and simply held each other tightly. Then they relaxed their embrace and looked into each other's eyes. Helen noticed how tired and anxious Charles looked, and he was alarmed by how pale and thin she was.

'Honey, I never realised how sick you were,' he said, feeling guilty. 'If I'd known I'd have come home – I'd have –'

'Don't, Charles, my dear,' said Helen, interrupting him. 'I didn't want to worry you needlessly. You had so much responsibility to bear in America. I didn't want to be an extra burden to you.'

He kissed her tenderly, amazed by her selfless love for him. 'Are you in a lot of pain, honey?' he asked.

'Most of the time. The doctors say I must have an operation,' said Helen fearfully.

Charles' face clouded with anxiety. He knew as well as she that an operation was the last resort. Without it she would certainly die; and yet even if she underwent surgery, she might not survive it. 'Do you have to have it done right away?' he asked.

'It must be soon. But I don't want to go into hospital just when you've returned. I want us to spend some time together first! I want you to have some happy memories of me, just in case. . .' She burst into bitter tears.

Charles took her in his arms again and tried to console her. 'Oh, honey, don't you worry, now,' he said. 'Everything will be just fine, you'll see. The Lord's looking after you – he'll see you through this operation.'

They next day they consulted Helen's doctor, who agreed that they could have two weeks together before the operation, but he insisted that after that Helen must go straight to a nursing home in London to undergo surgery. But in the event a mere five days passed before the pain in Helen's side became worse than ever, and it was clear that her life was now in danger. The London surgeon was sent for and the operation was performed there at 'Tennessee'.

As soon as the doctors had confirmed that Helen had to have the operation immediately, Charles sent telegrams to his family and to praying friends in America. One of these cables was sent to a prayer circle in a town in Iowa. One of its members was travelling in another part of the state when the message arrived, and so she could not be contacted by the other members, who speedily got down to serious prayer for Helen. However, the next day they received a letter from her saying that God had revealed to her that Helen Alexander was in special need, and so she was praying earnestly for her. There were many such friends praying for Helen during the operation. There was no doubt in her mind in later years that those prayers saved her life.

During the two weeks after the operation her life hung in the balance, and for a while after that her condition was complicated by a case of blood poisoning caused by the surgery. However, before too long she began to make a steady recovery. She and Charles now had to decide about their future. Helen needed months of rest, and could not possibly accompany Charles on the hectic round of missions which he and Dr Torrey had planned to conduct. Their long separation while Charles was in America had in the opinion of the doctors worsened Helen's condition, and another long time apart would without doubt delay her recovery from the surgery. Charles decided that he had to put his wife before his work and wrote to Dr Torrey, explaining with deep regret that he would be unable to take part in the forthcoming missions. He and Helen would spend a year cruising around the world, so that she could recover her health and strength.

6

A Cruise Around the World

While Helen and Charles set about making plans for their cruise around the world, a difficult problem arose at home. While Charles was in America, a slander had begun to circulate in the Birmingham area to the effect that he had another wife in the USA and had abandoned his English bride. The story eventually reached the ears of Charles' friends and supporters, who informed him of it when he returned from the States. At first he simply laughed off this ludicrous story, but he became concerned when he heard that people who had become Christians through the Bingley Hall mission in Birmingham were now being persecuted and ridiculed because of it. Cynics were sneeringly suggesting that the converts had been duped into a bogus Christian commitment by a hypocritical man who had become a bigamist. So Charles agreed that a special service should be held in Birmingham's Central Hall on 19th September at which the slander would be publicly refuted.

The hall was packed out on the night and Charles led the crowd in enthusiastic worship. Then eminent friends who had organised the Birmingham mission read out extracts from letters especially written by people who had known Charles all his life, testifying to his unswerving loyalty to Christ and his exceptional moral purity. After this Charles stood up in order to lead the crowd in another hymn, but the people could not be restrained from giving him a standing ovation which went on for many minutes. There was no doubt in their minds that the accusations against Charles were false, and with a humble smile he accepted their noisy vote of confidence in him. Finally, when he was able to quieten the crowd, he announced, 'I would never have said a word about this rumour if my friends had not said I might help some of the converts who are being persecuted. They told me there are some people who will never be satisfied till they hear me say I never married anyone before I married Miss Cadbury. It is beneath my contempt, but I want to let you know right now that I never did!' The crowd applauded loudly again. 'And I'm going to tell you another thing – I'm glad I didn't!' The crowd laughed and applauded yet again.

The evening had been a moving demonstration of the confidence which the Christian people of Birmingham had in Charles Alexander, and after this public refutation the ugly rumours died away. He was often subjected to such cruel attacks throughout his career by the cynical and the sceptical, since they found it impossible to believe that his life was really as pure and Christlike as it appeared to be. They wanted to believe that it was a hypocritical pretence. Another lie which sometimes circulated was to the effect that Charles and his colleagues were making large personal fortunes out of their evangelistic work. This slander, too, was absurd and laughable to anyone who knew the way in which they actually lived, because in reality theirs was a hand-to-mouth existence. They lived almost entirely off voluntary donations. There was never any opportunity for them to accumulate wealth, because as fast as they acquired it they spent it on the Lord's work, using it to cover their travelling and living expenses. However, God always provided them with what they needed, so that while they were never rich, they never lacked anything.

Once their domestic affairs were settled, Charles and Helen were able to set out on their cruise. Helen's sister

Margaret and her husband Neville had by that time been working as missionaries at Pakhoi in South China for about a year. As soon as Helen had proved to be truly on the mend after her operation her mother and Beatrice had gone out to see the Bradleys and the baby girl to whom Margaret had recently given birth. So Helen and Charles gladly decided to head straight for Pakhoi and join the rest of the family there. On 23rd November 1906 they sailed from Tilbury Docks in London aboard the S.S. *India*. Their prayer was that wherever they went on this cruise, they would be enabled to be good witnesses for Jesus Christ. Accompanying them on the voyage to Pakhoi was Hubert Gordon Thompson, a young medical doctor from Liverpool who was going out there to work with Neville Bradley.

The S.S. *India* stopped off at Port Said in Egypt, at Colombo in Ceylon, at Penang in Malaya, at Singapore and at Hong Kong. At each port Charles and Helen visited local missionaries, and during the long voyage they were given many opportunities to speak to their fellow passengers about Christ. At Hong Kong in early January they boarded a small Chinese steamer which then took them westwards around the coast of the mainland, through the Straits of Hainan and on to Pakhoi in the Gulf of Tonkin. Then there was a happy family reunion at the Bradleys' home. It seemed strange for them all to be together when they were so far from their native country and so far off the tracks usually beaten by Westerners in China.

Neville and Margaret eagerly showed Charles and Helen around the mission hospital and the nearby compounds for those who were suffering from leprosy. In the hospital the disease was treated by careful attention to cleanliness and by skilful surgery. In the compounds the patients all had jobs, each doing those tasks which he or she was best able to perform. Some grew food or prepared meals while others made craft products such as baskets which could be disinfected and sold. There was also a school and daily Bible classes, some of which were led by Christian patients. The disease and deformity which Helen and Charles saw at Pakhoi were terrible, but the examples of Christian faith, courage and joy which they also witnessed among the people there were amazing and deeply moving.

One incident made a particularly strong impression upon Helen. Some of the lepers had for the last eight years been printing one thousand copies of the Bible in Chinese, working on its books one by one. Finally the day came when they finished this herculean labour, and they then held a special praise meeting to celebrate. The finished books of the Bible had been stored in wooden boxes over the years, and now some of these were opened so that everyone could admire the work that had been done. But the printers were horrified to discover that white ants had got into the boxes and had eaten much of the paper. The work of years was ruined! But these Chinese Christians were undaunted by this setback, and soon afterwards started the entire printing project all over again.

One day the family decided to have a day off and enjoy a picnic in the nearby picturesque hills. Neville, Margaret, Beatrice and Charles went on horseback while Helen, her mother and Hubert Thompson went by a different route in Chinese carrying-chairs. When they were about halfway to their agreed rendezvous Helen heard the sound of a horse's hooves behind them. She turned in her chair and saw Beatrice galloping towards them with a very worried expression on her face. 'There's been an accident!' she called out. 'I'm afraid Charles is badly hurt. You must all come back to the mission compound!'

She galloped away again and immediately Helen and the others told their coolies to turn their chairs around and carry them back without delay. That return journey was a nightmare of anxiety for Helen, but throughout it she pleaded with God to preserve her beloved husband's life.

When they reached the Bradleys' home they found that the others had already arrived and had laid the unconscious Charles on a bed.

'What happened?' demanded Helen anxiously.

'Charles' horse was in the middle of a canter when it got its hoof stuck in a deep rut,' replied Neville. 'So he was thrown right off the saddle and landed flat on his face, getting a nasty blow on his right temple. He's been unconscious ever since. He was very fortunate to have fallen well away from the horse's hooves.'

Charles remained unconscious for two days, but thanks to the expert medical care which he received and the ceaseless prayers which were offered for him he eventually came around. Because of the blow to his head he suffered paralysis of his eyeball muscles for a few days and for some months after that was unable to turn his right eye. For weeks its pupil remained dilated, while that of his left eye shrank to a mere pinpoint. Eventually these difficulties disappeared and his eyesight was completely restored. However, for a few months he had to wear a strange-looking pair of spectacles which often aroused amusement, since one side of the frame had no glass in it, while the other was covered with a black patch!

In mid-February 1907 Charles, Helen, her mother and Beatrice took their leave of the Bradleys and went to Hong Kong, where Charles was booked to lead a big gospel meeting, having been persuaded to do so by local churchpeople when he and Helen were in Hong Kong while on their way to Pakhoi. On the evening of the meeting the Theatre Royal was packed out. There were many present who had never before attended any sort of Christian meeting, as well as many others who had previously seen Charles at work in his campaigns in the British Isles. It was the first time he had ever led a meeting without the assistance of a preacher such as

Dr Torrey. He looked rather comical wearing his odd spectacles, and the only musical accompaniment he had was his wife's piano playing which, although accomplished, lacked the sparkle of Robert Harkness' talent. However, Charles was a man so dedicated and surrendered to God that despite the less-than-perfect circumstances the Holy Spirit worked in a very powerful way at that meeting. For two hours he led the great crowd in song, in between the hymns giving short, practical talks on Christian living. Many of those present gave their lives to Christ. Helen felt nervous as she played the piano in front of that large audience, particularly since her health was not yet fully restored, but she was proud and happy to be assisting her husband in his ministry.

Five days later Helen and Charles sailed for Australia aboard the Japanese steamer *Nikko Maru,* having said farewell to Helen's mother and Beatrice, who were returning to Pakhoi for a while. As the ship steamed into Sydney Harbour and Helen and Charles watched from the rail of the upper deck he remarked, 'You know, honey, I can't help comparing arriving in Sydney now with my first visit here five years ago. Then I came here on my own, fresh from the American backwoods, about to start my work with Dr Torrey. Since then I've been all over the world. And now here I am again – this time bringing my wife with me!'

Helen squeezed his hand, sharing his feeling of joyful pride.

Few people in Australia knew that Charles was coming, but he and Torrey had made such a big stir there during their campaign in 1902 that once he and Helen had disembarked news of his arrival spread like wildfire and he was besieged with invitations to lead worship meetings. As a result their stay in Australia, which they had expected to last just a few days, stretched out to four whole weeks. Most of the meetings were held in Melbourne, but there were also some in the towns of Ballarat, Geelong and Bendigo.

Bendigo, a place famed for its gold mines, was the home of Charles' pianist Robert Harkness, and there he and his family treated the Alexanders to the warmest of Australian hospitality. The manager of one of the nearby mines was a Christian and invited them to visit it. Helen found the tour of the mine fascinating, if a little frightening at times. Dressed in overalls and hard hats and holding candles, they wended their way through the echoing passages six hundred feet below the surface, while the manager enthusiastically explained how everything worked. A couple of the miners they met down there were Christians and asked Helen and Charles to sing the *Glory Song*. They happily obliged, although Helen was slightly embarrassed by the experience – a mine seemed to her a strange place in which to sing! Charles, however, was hardly ever embarrassed – to him, any place was a good place in which to sing a gospel song.

As they sang a third miner joined them, singing the chorus as he emerged from one of the tunnels. 'How about another verse, sir?' the man asked Charles genially when they had finished.

Charles shook his hand. 'Are you a Christian man?' he asked in his disarmingly friendly way.

The big miner grinned a little sheepishly. 'No, sir, but you almost got me last night,' he said, referring to the evangelistic meeting in a nearby church which Charles had led the previous evening. 'The singing and the things you said made me shake from head to foot!'

'Do you believe in the Lord Jesus Christ?' asked Charles. 'Do you believe that he died for your sins?'

The man became thoughtful. 'Well now,' he said, 'I've thought hard about the things you said about Christ, sir, and yes, I think I do believe that he died for me.'

'Well, my friend, why don't you commit your life to him now?'

'What – here, sir? In this mine? It don't seem to me a proper place to do such a thing.'

'Anywhere is a good place to give your life to Christ,' Charles assured him with an encouraging smile. 'It makes no difference to God where you do it – whether it's on the ground or under it, whether inside a church or outside one. Won't you accept the Lord Jesus as your Saviour, right here, and live for him from now on?'

The miner became very solemn, and replied in a quiet though firm voice, 'Yes, I will.'

Then the visitors, the manager and the first two miners went down on their knees to pray for the man who had just committed his life to Christ. In a church service the next day, at Charles' request, he very simply but very movingly told the story of his conversion. He was just one of countless people all over the world who were brought to faith in Christ through Charles' work.

In early April 1907 Helen and Charles left the continent of Australia, bound for Vancouver in Canada. They stopped off on the way at Fanning Island – a beautiful coral reef which served as a cable station, inhabited by just a few dozen people – and at Honolulu in Hawaii. When they left Australia it had been autumn there, and it had been summer in Hawaii, but they reached Canada in North America's springtime, and to Helen's mind the profusion of daffodils, tulips and bluebells gave the season there an almost English quality.

From Vancouver they set out on a fascinating rail journey through the majestic Rocky Mountains, across the vast prairies of the Midwest to Chicago, and then on to New York. Helen's mother and Beatrice and three girl cousins who had joined them in South China were due to reach Vancouver just as Helen and Charles reached New York, so they waited there for the promised telegram telling of the safe arrival of their relatives on the west coast. A telegram did indeed arrive, but it did not bring the expected news. It informed a grief-sticken Helen that halfway between Yokohama and Vancouver her mother had suddenly died. Helen and Charles at once left New York and joined Beatrice and the others at Winnipeg in Canada, and there learned that Helen's mother had been thrown off her feet when the ship in which she was sailing suddenly lurched while she was ascending a steep stairway. Her head received a sharp blow when she fell, and she passed away later that same day.

Helen was stunned by the news. She had always been very close to her mother and knew that her death would leave a huge gap in her own life. She was so thankful that she had Charles. But in the midst of her grief she was also glad for her mother, because she had died a quick, painless death at the end of a happy, satisfying life. She also rejoiced for her because she knew that she was now in the presence of the Saviour whom she had loved and served for so many years, and because she was reunited at last with her beloved husband. The eight years since his death had been a lonely time for her, but now her loneliness was over. Together the family returned to England, and the body of Emma was buried in Birmingham beside that of her husband.

Charles had promised to help with some Bible conferences in America, so a few weeks later, at the end of July 1907, he made a return journey across the Atlantic. Meanwhile Helen and Beatrice got on with the sad task of breaking up the family home at 'Uffculme'. Beatrice moved into 'Tennessee', and a number of the servants at 'Uffculme' took up jobs there.

****

Charles returned from his commitments in America in September and found that he had some free time on his hands, since he had no other work planned. He was keen to begin a new evangelistic tour of the world, especially now that Helen was fully recovered from her operation. Both he and Dr Torrey had hoped to be able to renew their partnership, but to their mutual disappointment this now proved to be impossible. During Charles' voyage around the world with Helen, Torrey had continued with his own work and had been drawn back into the teaching ministry at the Moody Bible Institute in which he had been involved before his association with Charles, and had later accepted the position of Dean of the Bible Institute at Los Angeles. He was now committed to this work, so his globetrotting days were over. He and Charles always remained close friends, but their joint ministry was now over.

Ever since he became an evangelist Charles had made a point of emphasising to people everywhere the need to read and believe the Bible. He was convinced that knowing and living by the Word of God was the only way for individuals to truly grow in the Christian faith. He also believed that using Scripture was the best way of convincing people of their need of Christ, since the divinely inspired Word was 'living and active', as the writer of the Letter to the Hebrews had said, and often one verse of Scripture could change someone's life more powerfully than any amount of mere conversation could. Charles had often encouraged people to carry a New Testament with them at all times, so that it was always at hand for their own benefit and for use in witnessing to those who were not Christians. However, during the quiet weeks which he enjoyed at 'Tennessee' at the end of 1907 he began wondering if there might be some way in which he could give more force to this vital piece of advice. One day he was discussing this in the drawing room at home with Helen and George Davis, an American Christian writer who had come to England with Charles in September to help him write a book about worldwide evangelism.

'Charles,' said Helen, 'this idea of carrying the Bible with you everywhere reminds me of the Pocket Testament League which my friends and I set up at school.'

Charles turned to his wife with interest. 'What was the Pocket Testament League, honey?' he asked. 'You never mentioned it before.'

'It began when I and a few other Christian girls started trying to win some of our classmates to Christ,' replied Helen. 'Each of us always carried a New Testament to quote from when the need arose. We always tried to convince the girls by using Scripture alone, without resorting to clever arguments. Quite a number of girls became Christians through our witnessing and joined our group, so eventually we formed ourselves into a club and called it the Pocket Testament League. Its members had to promise to carry a New Testament with them always, to read a portion of it every day and to use it to win others to Christ. I think it carried on for a few years after we left school, but then it petered out.'

Charles was fascinated by this story. 'Well now, honey, that sounds like just the kind of thing we want right now!' he exclaimed. '"The Pocket Testament League" – I think I like the sound of that! I say we should revive it, and use it in our work in the future!'

Helen was quite amazed. 'Do you really think it would be helpful, Charles?' she asked. 'It was just something run by a few schoolgirls, after all.'

'Ah, but it worked, though, didn't it, honey? It worked because Scripture is powerful. Those young girls came to faith in Christ through hearing the Word, and they grew in faith because they had committed themselves to reading the Word regularly. Tell me, honey – did the girls who wanted to join your League have to be committed Christians already?'

'Yes, that's right,' answered Helen.

'H'mmm,' said Charles, reclining in his seat and staring at the ceiling, as he often did when thinking hard.

'So how do you think you can incorporate Helen's scheme into your present work, Charles?' asked George Davis, interrupting his thoughts.

'Well, I think I'd have to change it in one important respect if we were to use it in our work now,' he replied with animation. 'I think we wouldn't insist that in order to join people should already be committed Christians, but instead we would ask that having been given a copy of the New Testament, they should promise to carry it with them everywhere and to read a passage of it every day. That way, we'll get the Word of God into the lives of people who would otherwise never be exposed to it, and I believe God will use his Word to bring them to salvation.'

'So do you think you can use the League as a means of evangelism?' asked Helen.

'That's right, honey! If we can get people to read the Word, they'll get saved!'

'Do you really think that just reading Scripture can do it?' asked George. 'Don't you think people need to hear good gospel preaching and teaching as well?'

'Oh, yes, of course,' agreed Charles, 'and we should always encourage people to go and hear the Word of God preached. But there are vast numbers of people who have an antipathy to churches and to organised Christianity in general, maybe because they've not been impressed by what they've seen of church life in the past. I think the Pocket Testament League will be the ideal way of reaching people like that with the gospel.'

Davis was getting excited by the idea. 'Maybe you should test the scheme out on a small scale before you commit yourself to it in a big way,' he suggested.

'That's a good idea,' said Charles. 'Say, we could try it out on the streets around here! George, why don't you take a few days off from writing the book and go around with a bagful of testaments and try to get people to read them?'

'That suits me fine,' said George. 'I've been suffering from writer's cramp lately, anyway!'

Straight away Charles and George had some slips printed bearing a pledge to carry a testament everywhere and to read at least a chapter of it each day. They then pasted these onto the inside front covers of several dozen attractively illustrated little testaments.

And so it was that the next day George Davis could be seen wandering the streets around 'Tennessee' carrying a briefcase full of testaments. Early in the morning he struck up a conversation with a tall policeman at the top of Moor Green Lane.

'It's a fine morning, isn't it, officer?' he said.

'Yes, it certainly is – for November, at any rate,' replied the policeman. He had noticed George's accent and asked, 'Excuse me, but are you from America?'

'That's right,' replied George. 'I'm working with Charles Alexander, the evangelist. I expect you've heard of him.'

The policeman's face lit up with interest. 'Oh, yes, everyone's heard of Mr Alexander – he and Dr Torrey have made a big stir here in Birmingham, and all over the country, for that matter. And, of course, his name is well known in this area, since he and his wife live here.'

'Did you go to any of the meetings he and Dr Torrey held at Bingley Hall?' asked Davis.

'Well, no – that sort of thing's not really my cup of tea, if you know what I mean, although I've nothing against folk that do like it. Far from it.'

George fished a New Testament out of his briefcase. 'Would you like to have one of these?' he asked.

'What is it?' asked the policeman.

'Just a New Testament. It's yours, if you want it.'

'What, for free?'

'Yes, for free – but to have it you need to sign the pledge there on the inside cover.'

The policeman took the testament and examined it, delighted to be offered such an attractive little book. 'Well, thank you very much,' he said.

'And will you carry it with you all the time and read a chapter of it every day?' asked Davis.

'Yes, I certainly will,' promised the policeman, taking a pencil out of his pocket and signing the pledge.

'Well then, I hope you find it a blessing to you,' said George. 'I must be on my way now. Good day to you.'

84

That day he had many similar conversations with people on the streets, managing to give away about two dozen testaments. He eagerly continued the experiment for several days afterwards.

A month later, at the end of a small evangelistic meeting in a Mission Hall in Birmingham, Charles asked those who had made a decision to receive Christ as their Saviour that evening to come to the front of the hall. Immediately a tall, fine-looking man who had been sitting at the back stood up and walked boldly to the front, followed by a number of other people from different parts of the hall. Charles was impressed by the tall man's prompt decision and said to him, 'Brother, I don't usually ask this of people, but I would like to know what led you to decide for Christ. Would you mind telling us?'

The man pulled a little book from his pocket and held it up. 'It was this testament, sir, given to me a month ago,' he said. Then George Davis, who was also present that night, recognised the man as the policeman he had spoken to in Moor Green Lane, now dressed in plain clothes. Charles and George spoke to the man after the meeting and found out that he had quite simply read himself into God's kingdom.

This was a great encouragement to Charles, since it proved his belief that the Word of God had the power, without human interpretation or guidance, to lead a soul to salvation through Christ. Inspired by this success, he and George made a concerted effort in the coming weeks to evangelise other policemen from the local stations at Moseley and King's Heath, giving each of them a testament. During the next five months quite a number of them became Christians, and in one of the stations eight were converted. In later life one of these men was even to become an elder in the Presbyterian Church. Now more than ever Charles felt sure that the Pocket Testament League was going to be powerfully used by the Lord in the years ahead, and that it had to be a key element in his future evangelistic work.

7

A New Partner for Charles

Charles was now presented with a number promising possible ways in which to continue his evangelistic work, but he found it difficult to decide which was the right one. Whatever shape his future ministry was to take, he wanted to use the Pocket Testament League on a wide scale. He also wanted to fulfil the promise he had made to the Christian leaders of Australia while working there with Dr Torrey in 1902 to return for a new campaign. How should he bring about the realisation of these two aims?

By the end of November 1907 he was feeling increasingly sure that he should do it through a partnership with the American preacher, Dr J. Wilbur Chapman. The two men had been good friends since they first met in 1900, and Charles now felt that of all the preachers and teachers he knew, Chapman would be the most suitable to work with him in Australia. So by the end of December, when Charles went with Helen to meet Chapman in America, he had more or less decided that if Chapman would agree to accompanying him on the Australian campaign, he would take it as confirmation from God that the two of them should become partners.

Like Charles, Dr Chapman had been deeply influenced by the evangelist D. L. Moody. He had had a highly successful evangelistic preaching ministry in the Presbyterian Church but by 1907 he felt increasingly called to devote himself entirely to the interdenominational evangelism which was gathering pace in the USA at that time, so from his point of view the prospect of a partnership with Charles Alexander was ideal.

He had an unswerving belief in the Bible as the inspired Word of God, yet did not harshly condemn those Christian leaders whose belief in it was less sure. This gentleness of his was a far more persuasive way of bringing them to a full acknowledgement of the Bible's authority than a more aggressive attitude would have been. In private life as well as in the pulpit he had an attractively simple, genuine and sympathetic manner, and was always ready to feel for those who were suffering.

As a speaker he had the ability to stir and yet at the same time quieten an audience by his voice, which had a compelling, musical quality to it. He had a razor-sharp intellect and an astonishing gift for saying a great deal in a few well-chosen words. After a twenty-minute talk from him people often felt that they had heard an hour-long sermon, so stimulating was his preaching. One of his chief concerns was that the people who professed faith in Christ at campaign meetings should not be left to fend for themselves but should be encouraged to join live churches where they would be able to grow as Christians.

Charles spent January 1908 working with Chapman at various missions in America, and by the end of the month the two men were so impressed by each other's spiritual stature and highly effective working methods that they definitely agreed to become partners. Charles and Helen then went back to England for a short while to set their domestic affairs in order, after which they returned to America for the campaign which Charles was to conduct with Chapman in Philadelphia in March and April. The mission was organised according to the simultaneous system which Dr Chapman had developed in the course of his own evangelistic work in the past. The city was divided up into forty-seven districts in which over fifty evangelists and gospel singers were to work. Evangelistic meetings were held in three hundred churches every night, and there were also noonday meetings in the Garrick Theatre for business men and women. The district choirs had five thousand members altogether, and in addition there were five thousand personal workers, two thousand ushers, a thousand door-to-door evangelists and two hundred and fifty district leaders.

Charles and Dr Chapman found that they got on as a team even better than they had expected, and the campaign yielded substantial results. However, Chapman was increasingly coming to the conclusion that his simultaneous system of evangelism was too cumbersome, and so in subsequent missions he and Charles gradually adopted a simpler approach, focusing their work mostly upon large central meetings. These meetings were supplemented by various specialist activities such as prison-visiting and by a strong emphasis upon the Pocket Testament League. Chapman and Alexander took great numbers of testaments with them on their future campaigns. Each included a membership pledge to be signed inside the front cover, a brief explanation of how to become a Christian and a pledge of commitment to Christ inside the back cover. In countless thousands of cases people who signed the first pledge and then read the testament eventually came to the stage at which they were ready to sign the second pledge.

The revival hymns which Charles taught the crowds were whistled, sung and hummed all over the city. A new hymn written by Robert Harkness entitled *He will hold me fast* proved to be particularly popular.

One afternoon at a private gathering at the Lincoln Hotel the Pocket Testament League was formally presented to the evangelists working in the campaign, and was enthusiastically accepted by them. A few days later the League was officially launched at a special public meeting at the Academy of Music.

After the great Philadelphia campaign Charles and Dr Chapman held a brief mission in Norfolk, Virginia, where the meetings were well attended by sailors from the naval bases there. Many of them eagerly joined the Pocket Testament League.

After the Norfolk campaign Helen and Charles spent a happy week with the Alexander family at Knoxville, Tennessee, and from there joined Dr Chapman at Kansas City for some evangelistic meetings at the Presbyterian General Assembly. In early June 1908 Helen and Charles went to England for a brief stay at their home, only to return to the USA at the beginning of August, accompanied by Beatrice, an English cousin and Miss Perks, their secretary at 'Tennessee', all three of whom spent a month with them at the Bible conferences at Northfield and Winona Lake.

After that Helen and Charles were at Orilla in Canada for a two-week-long campaign in September, followed by a series of short conferences in Ohio, Kentucky and Tennessee. Finally there was a campaign at Burlington, Vermont, towards the end of November, and then they crossed the Atlantic for the sixth time that year! Charles had just four weeks to spend at 'Tennessee', and even during that time he was often away at meetings in various big towns in Britain. He and Helen enjoyed Christmas day together in their own home, which was a rare pleasure for them. Then he was off to America once again for campaigns with Dr Chapman in Richmond, Virginia and in Boston and Springfield, Massachusetts. Helen had to remain at home this time in order to prepare 'Tennessee' for their forthcoming long absence, since the much-heralded campaign in Australia was finally drawing near. She was to rejoin Charles in America later.

The campaign in Boston, from 26th January to 21st February 1909, was highly successful, despite widespread predictions that the city would not be set alight by revival as other places had been. It was a major centre of

Unitarianism, Christian Science, spiritism, Theosophy, Buddhism, devil-worship and other cults and superstitions, and the Christian churches there, living amidst such an oppressive spiritual atmosphere, were weary and lacking in life and zeal. Many of the ministers doubted the authority of the Bible. It was generally believed that no evangelistic effort could change the place, but through the Chapman–Alexander campaign God did what had previously seemed impossible. New life and vigour was injected into the churches, many half-hearted Christians rededicated themselves to their Lord and two thousand five hundred people were converted. Even the local newspapers were bowled over, each of them eventually devoting three or four pages every day to reports of the campaign. A number of the journalists became Christians. The Pocket Testament League made a big impact in the city and hundreds accepted testaments and signed pledges. The pastor of one of the Boston churches wrote:

> Mr Charles M. Alexander, with his beaming countenance, which seems to reflect the very love of his Lord, instantly wins the affection of the people he meets. His ardent temperament, splendid enthusiasm, and unquestioning consecration, give him a tremendous power over the audiences before whom he stands. He is nothing less than a genius in his abilities as a director, and gives power and pathos to the most ordinary musical composition. It would be impossible to conceive of two men more supplemental to each other than Dr Chapman and Mr Alexander. Each one needs the other for the largest effectiveness of his work.

Helen reached New York on 12th March, and she and Charles spent a quiet couple of days together there before beginning their journey to Australia. They sailed from Vancouver with Dr Chapman aboard the Japanese S.S. *Makaru* on 26th March 1909, having stopped off on their way across North America at conferences at Buffalo, Minneapolis and Winnipeg. Accompanying them was a large and gifted mission party.

It seemed strange to Helen to be crossing the Pacific, bound for Australia once again, when she and Charles had left there and sailed the ocean in the opposite direction just two years ago during her convalescent cruise around the world. Since then they had been all over North America and Great Britain, and she had lost count of the number of times they had crossed and recrossed the Atlantic. They had had little time to spend alone and scarcely any time at all at 'Tennessee', their own home in England. But Helen accepted all of this gladly. She had known when she became Charles' wife that theirs would be no ordinary marriage and that they would spend much of their time in the years to come either separated or travelling on account of Charles' evangelistic ministry.

She regretted nothing about her marriage. Charles was a wonderful, loving husband to her and she found great joy and satisfaction in being able to look after him and support him in his work for the Lord. She also continued to play her own part in winning souls to Christ at the missions. It was fascinating and exciting to be able to travel to so many far-flung corners of the globe, meeting the people and witnessing the growth of the Church in so many different places.

Now that she was completely recovered from her operation, she was once again full of the enthusiasm and zest for life which had always been one of her traits. This was one of the reasons why she and Charles were such ideal life companions: they were both constantly brimming over with energy. People of more limited strength could never have lived life at such an astonishing pace as they did. If anything Helen was even more energetic than Charles. Sometimes he couldn't keep up with her!

On the journey across the Pacific the S.S. *Makaru* called at Honolulu in Hawaii and at Suva in the Fijian Islands, reaching the shores of Australia on 17th April. Two days later the party disembarked at Sydney and then travelled another five hundred miles by train to Melbourne for the first phase of the planned continent-wide campaign. Here the Australian people – overjoyed that at long last Charles Alexander, who with Dr Torrey had in 1902 so blessed the spiritual life of their nation, had returned to them – gave the mission party the very warmest of welcomes. They instantly accepted Dr Chapman. So great had been their regard for and trust in Charles that they had left in his hands the choice of the speaker who would accompany him on the Australian mission, and when for the first time they heard Chapman speak they immediately knew that he was God's chosen man for this campaign, just as much as Charles was.

On their first day in Melbourne there were a number of preliminary meetings, in which the leaders and organisers of the campaign heartily welcomed the mission party. Then the campaign started in earnest, and for the next month every part of the city of Melbourne was stirred by it. There were packed noon and evening meetings in the Town Hall during the first two weeks, while the King's Theatre and other halls and churches were often filled by subsidiary services. During the last two weeks there were daily evening meetings in the city's great Exhibition Building and a number of afternoon services.

The day of the first midday meeting in the Town Hall happened to be a public holiday, so the building was packed out. Ernest Naftzger, the American soloist who assisted Charles in leading worship, had not yet arrived at the hall when the meeting was due to start, so to get the ball rolling Charles asked his secretary, E. H. Bookmyer, to come up to the dais and sing a verse of the hymn, *He will hold me fast*. Bookmyer's voice wasn't an outstanding

92

one, but he sang powerfully and movingly. When he had finished Charles, smiling, said to the crowd, 'Now, no one here has any excuse for not singing that song, because if my secretary can sing it, anybody can!' The crowd laughed, showing that they were in a relaxed, holiday mood.

Then Charles gave them some singing tuition. 'Cut your words off short,' he said, 'just as if you were speaking them.' The crowd followed his orders obediently and sang the words of *He will hold me fast* vigorously and clearly. The time passed swiftly as Charles led the crowd in singing one hymn after another.

Then Dr Chapman gave a short, powerful address on the subject of sin, showing the people how to overcome it by having faith in Christ as their Saviour and by living in the power of the Holy Spirit. The crowd was hushed as he described the power of sin and showed how even the strongest person failed to keep the commandments. Only spiritual rebirth through Christ could save an individual from the slavery of sin, and only the power of the indwelling Holy Spirit could enable that person to live a holy life. Chapman took a penknife from his pocket, held it between finger and thumb and let it drop to the floor. He picked it up and did the same thing again. He picked it up once more, pointed at it and said, 'I command you not to fall!' But when he released it, again it fell to the floor. Once more he commanded it not to fall, and once more it fell. Then he took a magnet from his pocket and held it to the knife blade. Keeping hold of the magnet, he let go of the knife yet again. This time, of course, it did not fall. Then he explained that without Christ, a person is in the same predicament as the penknife. God commands us not to fall into sin, but we are unable to obey him. But just as the power of the magnet overcomes gravity's power over the knife, so too the power of Christ in our lives can overcome the downward pull of sin. A thrill of understanding went through the crowd as he quoted from Romans chapter 8:

'The law of the Spirit of life in Christ Jesus hath made me free from the law of sin and death.' He pronounced the benediction over the people, who then went away inspired and challenged by the truths they had heard, many of them now more determined to live holy lives by the power of the Holy Spirit.

All the meetings held at Melbourne were remarkable and changed the lives of those who attended. This was how Helen was in future years to recall one of the meetings which took place towards the end of May:

At a quarter to seven in the evening the crowds started to pour into the Exhibition Building like a great river of people, dividing into streams. One stream surged up the central aisle and filled the ground floor; other streams swept up the staircases to the galleries above. Just twenty minutes after the opening of the doors all the seats were full! The doors then had to be closed, and hundreds of disappointed people were unable to get in.

For another twenty minutes the crowd waited, in a happy mood, looking forward to the evening's singing; they were also in a rejoicing mood, yearning to worship God. At twenty-five minutes past seven Charles bounded up onto the dais in the centre of the hall, welcomed by thunderous applause and cheering from the enormous crowd. He waved in greeting to them, and once they had quietened down just a little he cried out with pleasure, 'We are to have a three hours' sing! Get ready for a long, hard, delightful evening! We are all going to join the choir!' Another surge of happy applause.

He raised his hands for silence, and prayed simply and fervently, dedicating the evening to God. Then the whole crowd stood up to sing *Abide with me*. At the end of the hymn Charles called out, 'The last phrase in just a whisper!' and the crowd obeyed. Then the choir followed this with a full-volumed 'Amen'. The effect was beautiful and deeply moving.

94

A few in the crowd started calling out the numbers of hymns they wanted to be sung. With good humour Charles replied, 'Wait a minute. I'll tell you when you can have your choice. We're going to learn a new chorus while we are fresh. There's enough in this to save any man, no matter how deep in sin.'

The song was *I believe, I believe on the Son of God*. The sopranos of the choir sang it first, and then the whole choir, while the audience listened. Charles turned to the crowd and asked, 'Now are you ready for it?' They didn't seem too sure, so Charles, with the quick, intelligent flexibility which was one of the hallmarks of his public ministry, immediately adopted another plan. Pointing to one of the Australian officials he asked, 'Don't you think there's enough in that chorus to save any man?'

'Yes, I do,' the man replied.

'Then give a Bible to the first volunteer who will sing it.'

The man nodded, and a murmur of anticipation passed through the crowd. Two ladies stood up and volunteered to sing. The first one was very nervous, but did her best, and the second one sang the song well. Charles declared that both ladies should get Bibles, and then made the whole crowd sing the song. The words, 'I believe, I believe on the Son of God' resounded in the great hall, their power touching the hearts of the singers and changing their lives as they did so. A moving and thrilling sense of genuine worship of Christ filled the hall. 'Glory!' cried a Salvation Army officer near the dais, his eyes shining with joy.

Charles then noticed a lady in a wheelchair at the front of the hall. 'And what hymn would you like, ma'am?' he asked her kindly.

'Can we sing *There's power in the blood*, please?' she said.

Charles smiled. 'Yes, let's sing that one!' he said eagerly. 'How we used to make this old building ring with that hymn seven years ago! Sing the chorus, choir!' he commanded. 'Tell these people that there is "power, power, wonder-working power in the blood of Christ!"'

The choir burst into song, and the word 'power' echoed repeatedly around the hall. Then the whole crowd sang the song. Through its words thousands present that night gained a new, clearer understanding of the truth that the blood of Jesus Christ has the power to cleanse the human heart from sin and bondage.

Charles then announced that Ernest Naftzger would sing *The Ninety and Nine*, a hymn based on the parable of the lost sheep. The soloist's strong, beautiful voice carried the song to the furthest corners of the hall. The passion with which he sang mounted with each verse until the culmination of the final line: 'Rejoice, for the Lord brings back His own.' Then the choir sang the word 'rejoice' again and again, and then the whole last line: 'Rejoice, *rejoice*, REJOICE, for the Lord brings back His own.' Next Charles told the right-hand gallery to sing the line; then the left-hand gallery; then the people under the dome in the centre of the building; then the ones in the galleries beyond it. Finally he asked everyone to stand, and they sang it in unison with all the sincerity and passion their hearts could muster: 'REJOICE, for the Lord brings back his own.'

That evening was a time of exalted worship which none of those who experienced it would ever forget; and yet it was just one of many, many such occasions in Charles Alexander's career. As she watched her husband leading the vast crowds in praise to God, Helen's heart would always swell with pride in him and love for him, and she would give thanks to God for making her the wife of a man whom he had chosen to use in order to bless countless lives the world over.

The farewell meeting in the Exhibition Building at the close of the Melbourne mission was in some ways the most notable event of the whole month. More than nine thousand people flocked to say goodbye to Charles and Dr Chapman, some five hundred ministers among them. The singing that day was the best yet, and it was with real regret that the mission party said goodbye to the people of Melbourne. Once the meeting was over they rushed to the railway station, reaching it only just in time to catch the train to Sydney, where the next phase of the great Australian campaign was to take place.

As was the case with Melbourne, the whole of Sydney, including its many suburbs, was electrified by Chapman and Alexander and the campaign held there was the start of a revival which swept through the whole of New South Wales. As in 1902, Sydney's huge Town Hall proved to be too small to accommodate all those who wanted to attend the meetings, so often four or five nearby churches were filled with the overflow crowds. On the last Sunday of the month-long mission the crowds of people waiting to enter the Town Hall were so enormous and so dense that the police were gravely concerned that there would be accidents and injuries, so in order to get some of the people off the streets they ordered the doors to be opened at five o'clock instead of seven, when the meeting was due to start. When Charles and Dr Chapman heard this they decided to start the meeting early, fearing that a two hour-long wait would make the people in the Town Hall restless and unmanageable. They began at five-thirty, and after an hour of worship they opened some of the doors so as to allow the crowd out. Then a whole new crowd of people who had been waiting patiently outside was admitted for an unscheduled second service!

After Sydney the mission party had a long but interesting northward journey through Queensland to Brisbane, where they held a two week-long campaign. This was followed by a month's evangelistic work in the Philippine Islands and brief missions in Ballarat and Bendigo. Then there were some final services of farewell in Melbourne.

As Charles and Dr Chapman prepared to leave Australia the leaders of the churches there pleaded with them to return to the continent in three years' time. The two Alexander campaigns which, had so far been conducted in the country had stirred its spiritual life to the core and had fanned the flames of revival, but the inspiring ministry of Alexander and Chapman would still be greatly needed in the future. They promised to give the request very serious consideration.

Throughout the Australian campaign the Pocket Testament League, promoted at all the meetings, continued to grow and flourish at an astonishing rate. George Davis had accompanied Charles to Australia and had worked tirelessly for the League there. He often went out onto the streets to enlist people, and had particular success with policemen and tramcar workers. In both Melbourne and Sydney groups of League members were formed which in the years to come won great numbers of people into God's kingdom. Helen was deeply gratified that her schoolgirl efforts in evangelism were after all these years bearing so much fruit in places so distant from her childhood home.

On 11th August 1909 the mission party sailed from Sydney harbour aboard the Japanese steamer, S.S. *Kumano Maru*, bound for the coast of China, where they would begin the missionary tour of the Far East which had been planned to follow the Australian campaign. The sea voyage served as a much-needed rest after the intensely hard work of the past four months, but they still found the energy and enthusiasm to witness to their fellow passengers and to the crew, using the Pocket Testament League as an evangelistic tool. Charles, Helen and the others spoke to the crew through an interpreter. Almost all of the officers accepted Japanese testaments and signed the pledge. The ship's barber, Nakai, was converted and became an enthusiastic member of the League, keeping in touch with George Davis for years afterwards.

In cities all over Asia missionaries were looking forward to a visit by the Chapman–Alexander team, and meetings had been arranged in each place both for the nationals and for the westerners, the majority of whom were as much in need of hearing the gospel message as were the native people. First of all the party visited missionaries at Hong Kong at the end of August. They were joined there by Beatrice Cadbury, who had been staying with the Bradleys at Pakhoi and would now accompany the party on its travels in Asia. After Hong Kong they had a ten-day-long stay at Shanghai. Charles and Dr Chapman had some fascinating meetings there with Chinese pastors, many of whom became very interested in the Pocket Testament League and promised to introduce it into their churches. Over the years that were to follow Helen and Charles were to receive many amazing reports of great spiritual revivals which were sparked off by the 'Sleeve Testament League'. It was called this because the Chinese people carried their testaments in their sleeves, since their traditional garments had no pockets.

From Shanghai the party moved on to the famous and ancient city of Nanking, where further rewarding contacts were made with missionaries and national Christians. Then there was a marvellous five-hundred-mile-long river voyage up the great Yangste-Kiang to Hankow, and then a railway journey of six hundred miles to Peking. After a brief stay at Tientsin they moved on to Korea, where they spent some busy weeks in October. This country was open to the West and was not yet under the oppressive sway of Japan, so the young Church there was growing very rapidly. From Korea the party crossed over to Japan and spent three-and-a-half weeks visiting Christians in the cities of Kobe, Osaka, Kyoto, Nagoya, Yokahama and Tokyo.

In all the places in Asia the mission party visited they succeeded in giving inspiration and encouragement to the Christians there and in bringing souls to faith in

Christ. One of the incidents which Helen remembered most vividly happened in the Japanese city of Nagoya. During a crowded evening meeting in a church there Charles felt guided by the Holy Spirit to give the people a song to sing in their own language. So he asked a few of the missionaries to come with him into the vestry and there got them to translate for him a chorus which had been very effective in campaigns all over the world. Its words were very simple, but time and again God had used them to touch hearts and change lives:

> I surrender all,
> I surrender all,
> All I have I bring to Jesus,
> I surrender all.

Charles asked the missionaries to write out the Japanese words phonetically in Roman characters so that he could pronounce them. He tried reading the words out once, and the missionaries assured him that the people would understand him. Satisfied with this, he returned to the pulpit with the chorus and through an interpreter told the people that he wanted to teach it to them. He then boldly started to sing the song, following the phonetic syllables which had been written out for him. Smiles of surprise and delight instantly appeared on the faces of the people, and Charles too was delighted when they all bowed low to him to signify that they had clearly understood what he had sung. Then the whole church took up the song, and the Japanese people sang it with great gusto. They were deeply touched that the American evangelist had gone to the trouble of singing to them in their own language, and so the song meant all the more to them. There followed a few moments of prayer, which were suddenly interrupted by the sound of a Japanese voice coming from the gallery. It belonged to a little man with a big moustache who seemed to be pleading for something, his voice rising and falling plaintively while tears streamed down his face.

'What is he saying?' Charles asked one of the missionaries.

'He's saying that the wonderful song has laid hold of him and he wants permission to come down to the front of the meeting and tell his story,' whispered the missionary.

'Tell him to come at once,' said Charles.

Moments later the man walked down the aisle, his Japanese shoes click-clacking on the hard floor. He turned to face the people and bowed low, his head dropping below the level of his stiffened knees, where his hands rested. The people bowed to him in a similar fashion. Then he told his story, with great fervour, while one of the missionaries interpreted his speech for Charles, Helen and the others. The man was a blacksmith and had always been hostile to the Christian gospel, which he had heard from missionaries. Ten years ago one of them had given him a Bible, but he had torn it to pieces and had vowed that he would never enter a place of Christian worship. However, for some reason he had felt compelled to go to the meeting at the church that night, and he now realised that he had been drawn there by the power of God. He said that the sermon preached earlier had challenged him and that when *I surrender all* had been sung he had received a revelation of Jesus and had immediately accepted him as Saviour and Lord. He told how he was often drunk and violent and frequently beat his wife in fits of rage, but he said he had now decided to go home and start a new life, endeavouring to be a good husband to his wife and a good father to his three children.

This was just one of the many examples of lives being changed by Christ which the mission party witnessed during their travels in Asia. Charles later received confirmation in a letter that the blacksmith's whole family had become Christians and had joined a Japanese church.

After a brief stay in Yokohama the party divided at last. George Davis, at the request of the missionaries in Korea, returned there to further promote the Pocket Testament League, which had caused a marvellous revival. Helen's sister Beatrice returned to the Bradleys in Pakhoi, while Helen, Charles, Dr Chapman and all the others sailed for Vancouver on 15th November aboard the *Empress of China*. As the ship steamed out of Yokohama harbour Helen felt that another chapter of her busy and exciting life with Charles had ended, and she wondered what further challenges and joys God had in store for them in the future.

8

Summers at 'Tennessee'

It was early April 1910. The gardens of 'Tennessee' were graced with all the colourful and fragrant finery of spring. The driveway to the house also looked magnificent, as it had been decorated with festoons of laurel and hundreds of little flags, which fluttered in the breeze. A grocer's boy on a bicycle passed through the gates and braked to a screeching halt in the driveway, astonished by the sight he saw. Then he rode up to the house and knocked at the kitchen door in order to deliver his goods.

'Are yer expectin' Royalty, then?' he asked the cook when she opened the door.

She laughed happily. 'No, lad – not Royalty, but the next best thing as far we're concerned. Mr and Mrs Alexander are coming home today!'

'Where have they been, then?'

'Oh, all over the world, lad – Australia, China, America. They've been away for sixteen months.'

Not long after this a hansom-cab rounded a bend in Moor Green Lane and turned into the driveway. In the cab were Helen and Charles, exhausted after their long journey but thrilled to be coming back to 'Tennessee' at last. As they neared the house Charles put his head out of the window and whistled loudly. 'Hey, everybody! We're home!' he called.

A moment later the front door opened to reveal a group of happy-faced girls and women, all dressed in white caps and aprons. From a side gate three of the gardeners emerged to greet their master and mistress.

Helen and Charles stepped out of the cab and shook hands with the household staff, exchanging warm greetings with them. It was good to be home!

The mission party had reached Vancouver at the end of November 1909, and after attending a few short conferences while crossing North America they had spent the first three months of the new year at missions in New England and Ohio. The time spent in Ohio was to be especially significant for Dr Chapman, since it was while he was there that he met Mabel Moulton, from Providence, Rhode Island, who was later to become his wife.

Helen and Charles had gone back to England ahead of the rest of the party. A couple of days after their arrival at 'Tennessee' Beatrice returned from China, having travelled by way of Siberia, Russia and Europe. A few days later Dr Chapman and eleven others of the party joined them at the house for a brief holiday. Then, after just four days of rest, the whole mission party went back to their work, beginning a month-long campaign in Cardiff. After that they returned briefly to the States to attend the Presbyterian General Assembly in Atlantic City. While there Charles was taken seriously ill with appendicitis. However, he soon recovered sufficiently to be able to make the return journey across the Atlantic in order to attend the World's Missionary Conference in Edinburgh in June 1910.

After this Charles and Helen decided to have a holiday alone together, partly because his problem with his appendix kept recurring, which meant that he needed rest. A two-week-long stay at the Lizard in Cornwall did them both the world of good. Helen had often told him how beautiful the rugged Cornish coast was, and now that he had seen it for himself he loved it as much as she.

Now, for the first time in years, Helen and Charles could look forward to spending a whole summer together at home at 'Tennessee', since he had no further commitments until the autumn. However, the trouble with his appendix worsened in July, and it became necessary for him to have an operation similar to the one Helen had had. The thought of undergoing surgery was always a sobering one in those days, because operations were by no means as safe then as they are now. However, Charles trusted God with all his heart and believed that in his love and mercy he would protect his life. Before the operation Helen and Charles prayed together that God would guide the surgeon's hand and that the operation would be fully successful. He gave a note to his wife as they walked together to the temporary operating theatre which had been set up in their home. 'Please read this while the doctors are at work, honey,' he said. Helen stayed with Charles while he was given the anaesthetic, holding his hand the whole time. Then she left her husband in the care of the surgeons and went to an adjacent room to pray. She took out the note he had given her. It read:

My precious Helen, I love you, and I can never tell you the hundred thousand ways you help and make me. It is heaven to live with you . . . You are my best adviser. When I think of you, honey, I always think of the Scripture verse, 'Exceeding abundantly above all that we can ask or think.' You have made it so easy to approach this solemn event.

The operation was successful and uncomplicated, and Charles quickly made a full recovery. Not even the weakness and pain he suffered at this time could quench his desire to win souls to Christ, and through his gentle witness both of the nurses who looked after him during his recovery became Christans and joined the Pocket Testament League! During the years of Helen's and Charles' marriage many other people were similarly blessed and touched by God simply through being with them and absorbing the joyful, loving Christian atmosphere which existed at 'Tennessee'. The Alexanders did not confine their evangelism to organised missions but even looked upon their home life as an opportunity for winning people to Christ.

Charles' convalescence was completed by two more idyllic weeks in Cornwall, after which he and Helen welcomed Dr Chapman and his bride, who had just been married in the States, at 'Tennessee'. Charles was delighted that his colleague's bachelorhood was at last ended and that God had provided him with such a fine wife. He knew from his own experience how lonely work such as theirs could be without the companionship of a spouse. Over the years ahead Helen and Mabel were to enjoy a good friendship since, being both married to globetrotting evangelists, they had much in common.

Helen and Charles spent the rest of that summer peacefully at home. In fact it turned out that the following three summers were to be spent the same way. They were to become golden memories for Helen. It was exciting to be able to serve God in an evangelistic ministry all over the world, but it was also delightful to be just a husband and wife, enjoying the pleasures and comforts of home. These periods of quiet gave them a chance to recover from the exertions of their busy lives, and also provided Charles with much-needed free time in which to work on the hymn books which he produced for use in his campaigns.

'Tennessee' was inundated during these summers by a constant stream of visitors, most of them missionaries whom Helen and Charles had met on their travels around the world. Over the years there must have been hundreds of Christian workers who were encouraged and strengthened in their faith by the happy, godly environment which they found at the Alexanders' home. It was readily apparent to all who met them that Helen and Charles were people who loved Christ with all their hearts, and that as a result his love filled them and flowed out to other people.

In his public life Charles was a man who radiated Christian love and joy, and this was no less the case in his private life at home. Time and again visitors at 'Tennessee' found that the vitality and exuberance of his faith was not a mere religious act which he put on for the benefit of the crowds at evangelistic meetings, but was just as real at home as it was in a great gospel service. Years later one of these visitors wrote to Helen:

> Do you know that when I first came to 'Tennessee' I almost dreaded coming, lest I should be disappointed, for I loved and admired Charles so much, and I had so often been disappointed by those whom I saw on platforms. The first thing I noticed in the drawing-room was the little motto *Each for the other, and both for God.* I soon found that it was true, and Charles in the home was an infinitely bigger man to me than even Alexander on the platform. He was never once a disappointment to me.

'Tennessee' was happy, stimulating place in which to stay as a guest. There was always song, laughter and hectic activity going on. Charles was usually busy with his work in his Den, while Helen ran the household with the amazing energy and perfectionism that was characteristic of her. From her childhood she had been surrounded by servants and so was used to giving orders. Sometimes this attitude would spill over into her treatment of her guests, but they took it with good humour because they loved and admired her so much. Although she came from a wealthy background, there was not the least hint of snobbishness or arrogance about Helen. She was accustomed to wielding authority in her home and to expressing her views frankly, and yet there was an endearing humility about her. She never forgot that all people were equal in the sight of God, whether rich or poor, mistress or servant.

All the household staff at 'Tennessee' were Christians and had the highest regard for their master and mistress, not only as employers but also as fellow believers. Of course, the nature of the relationship between them inevitably meant that a certain distance had to be maintained, but despite that the Alexanders and their staff enjoyed an understanding based upon loyalty to their mutual heavenly Master.

Both Helen and Charles were ardently teetotal and also disapproved of smoking, but the atmosphere at 'Tennessee' was so convivial that the guests never noticed the absence of alcohol or tobacco. In any case, most of them, being Christians, would have held the same views as the Alexanders on this subject.

Helen was deeply fulfilled by her marriage to Charles. Their tender, passionate love for each other was enriched and given larger meaning by their mutual love for Christ. Because Christ was the greatest love in each of their lives, they were able to love each other more than they ever could have done otherwise. Daily Helen gave thanks to God for her husband and prayed that he would change and purify them both by the power of his Holy Spirit, so that their lives would increasingly demonstrate and radiate the life and love of Jesus.

Helen felt that she had much to be grateful for. Her one regret was that so far their marriage had not been blessed with children, even though they had hoped and prayed for a family right from the start. But perhaps their prayers would be answered in the fullness of time. Both she and Charles loved children, and their hearts ached whenever they met a family which had little ones. The pain they felt drove then to pray all the more and to surrender to God their desire to have children of their own. It was a hard prayer to pray, but they told God they were prepared to remain childless if that were his perfect will for them.

In the summer of 1910 Helen and Charles bought from the 'Uffculme' estate the 'Tea Sheds' which Richard Cadbury had erected in the grounds of the house as places in which to provide refreshments for the annual summer picnics of the Birmingham Sunday schools and Mothers' Meetings. The Alexanders converted one end of the sheds into two comfortable rooms, one called the Den and the other called the West Room. In the Den Charles kept his extensive library of hymn books, his remarkable collection of lantern slides and his many albums of photographs and press cuttings of the campaigns in which he had been involved. Many new hymns were composed by Charles and his assistants around the piano in the Den, and hundreds of other hymns, both old and new, were criticised, discussed and tried out in preparation for forthcoming missions and the production of new hymnbooks. Often the sound of singing would drift from the Den out to the nearby road, and intrigued passers-by would stop and listen.

Charles loved to be surrounded by young assistants, and there was always a group of them with him during the summers of 1910 to 1914, many of them Americans and Australians. In the West Room his 'boys' beavered away enthusiastically at the administration and publicity associated with the campaigns. To begin with the boys lived at 'Tennessee' or at nearby lodgings, but later Charles rented a furnished house in order to provide a real home for them. Since 'Tennessee' had been named after his home state in America, he thought it would be a good joke to name this new annex 'Kentucky', after one of the states adjoining Tennessee, and henceforth its residents were known as Kentuckians. They often ate with Helen and Charles at 'Tennessee' and sometimes they even entertained them at 'Kentucky'. Many were the mornings when the young men could be seen hurrying along the road to the Alexanders' house for breakfast, buttoning their jackets and straightening their ties as they ran. Many were the happy evenings they all spent together singing old and new gospel songs, telling stories, recalling the excitements and achievements of past campaigns all around the world and thinking about new missions in the future.

For Helen and Charles the pleasant summer of 1910 ended with a joyful piece of news. Helen was pregnant at last. She was so happy that she was going to be able to give a child to the man she loved and that at last her strong desire to be a mother was to be fulfilled. In the coming months many people noticed that Charles seemed even more bright and joyful than usual and were delighted when they heard that it was because he was expecting to be a father.

So it was with an added sense of joy and thanksgiving that they set out for America at the beginning of October, bound for the great city of Chicago, where a major campaign had been organised. The crowds at the meetings were immense, but because of the cumbersome nature of the simultaneous plan upon which the mission had been organised, the permanent results were not as great as Charles and Dr Chapman had hoped they would be. The Chicago mission was further proof to them that a centralised approach was generally more effective. There followed a short mission in December at Fort Wayne, Indiana, after which Helen and Charles spent Christmas in Columbus, Ohio with Charles' brother Homer (now the pastor of a Presbyterian church there), his wife and their three-year-old daughter.

The first two months of 1911 were taken up with campaigns in Toronto in Canada and Brooklyn in New York. Then in March the mission team returned to the British Isles for a month-long campaign in Swansea, followed by conferences in Belfast, Leeds and Birmingham and a mission in Shrewsbury.

By the time summer had come around again, Helen was due to give birth. In June the nation celebrated the coronation of King George V, and about a week later the household at 'Tennessee' buzzed with excitement as Helen went into labour. Charles was almost beside himself with joyful anticipation, mingled with anxiety about Helen's safety. He had wanted to stay with her during the labour, but such a thing was unheard-of in those days, so he was obliged to entrust his wife into the hands of the midwives. Several of his 'boys' kept him company throughout this anxious day, spending much of the time praying with him for Helen and the child.

Sadly, the labour proved to be a difficult one, and despite their best efforts the midwives could not successfully deliver the baby. Charles and his friends began to become worried, and prayed all the harder. Finally, after Helen had been in labour for eight hours, one of the midwives came to the drawing-room, where they were all anxiously awaiting news. From the expression of concern on her face Charles instantly perceived that all was not well.

'Mr Alexander, the baby has been delivered at last,' she said. 'It's a boy. But I'm afraid he's very weak.'

'How – how about Mrs Alexander?' stammered Charles.

'She's been exhausted by the long labour, sir, but she will recover.'

'And what about the baby? Will he live?'

'We can't say for sure, sir. The next few hours will tell.'

Immediately Charles went to see the child, who was being cared for by the midwives in a room adjoining Helen's. He looked so small and frail. Poor little boy, thought Charles, to have such a difficult start to life. And yet as he looked down at the tiny face, its bruised eyelids firmly shut, he smiled with fatherly pride and joy. 'Oh, heavenly Father,' he silently prayed with all his heart, 'please let our son live. You have given him to us – in return we dedicate him to you. Please let him live!'

After just a moment with the child, he went to see his beloved wife. She lay prostrate in her bed, looking utterly drained of energy. He took her hand and held it tightly, feeling her fingers grip his in response.

'My darling, thank God you're all right,' he said softly. 'The boys and I have been praying for you and the baby all day.'

Helen's voice was a hoarse whisper: 'The baby? . . .'

'He's going to be fine, honey – just fine,' Charles assured her, wishing that he felt as sure as he was trying to sound.

After a few moments she succumbed to her utter exhaustion and fell asleep.

Tragically, the child, weakened by the prolonged trauma of the labour, died within the hour. As soon as Charles heard he went to his wife again. She was asleep when he entered her room. He sat and waited for her to wake, wanting to be the one who told her the news.

When she awoke she immediately saw the expression upon his face and knew the truth. Tears welled up in her eyes and she wanted to cry out loud, but her exhaustion prevented her. He took her hand and kissed her cheek.

'Oh, Charles!' she cried, trying to rise from her bed. He took her in his arms and held her tightly for a long time.

After a while she whispered, 'The Lord gave, and the Lord hath taken away. Blessed be the name of the Lord.' Charles hugged her even tighter, loving her for the depth and strength of her faith in their Lord, even in this, one of the very hardest of life's trials.

Soon her weariness triumphed over sadness and she again fell into a deep sleep. Then Charles went to a disused bedroom at the top of the house and there wept and prayed, praising God despite this heart-rending tragedy, thanking him for preserving the life of his beloved Helen.

She physically recovered from the experience within a few weeks, but the emotional damage took much longer to heal. The feeling of bereavement and disappointment was almost unbearable. And, even worse, she felt that she was a failure as a woman, since she had been unable to give Charles a child. But he did everything he could to assure her that what he wanted from her even more than a family was her wifely love and companionship. He inspired her by the selfless attitude he took, devoting himself more than ever to her and to his work for God. He never allowed himself to wallow in self-pity and lived out the Bible's command to praise and thank God in all situations. Only those who knew how much he loved children and how strongly he had wanted to be a father could appreciate how hard this experience had been for him.

Helen and Charles continued to hope to be able to start a family, but this was not to be. The doctors said they saw no reason why Helen should not be able to conceive and give birth again, but it never happened. In the end Helen and Charles came to believe that in his wisdom God prevented them from having a family so that they could devote themselves fully to the task of bringing souls to Christ. They accepted this with the joy that comes from true faith in and devotion to God and lavished the parental love with which they were both well endowed upon those they met in the missions, upon the many friends who came to 'Tennessee' and upon Helen's many young nephews and nieces. Their childlessness was the only part of their marriage which caused them sorrow. And yet this sorrow did not drive them apart but brought them closer together, since it was a pain which they fully shared.

There were two other sorrowful events in the family that summer. Homer Alexander's wife died suddenly after an operation, leaving him with two little girls to look after. (He and his daughters later went to live with his mother near Detroit.) Also Arthur, the ten year-old son of Helen's brother Richard, died in a tragic accident at school. He had visited 'Tennessee' just a few months before this and had eagerly joined the Pocket Testament League. He had faithfully carried the testament which his Uncle Charles had given him and had the book in his pocket when he died. He had become a keen Christian and had persuaded many of his classmates to join the League.

But there were also sunshine in the Alexander home in the summer of 1911, because Helen's sister Beatrice became engaged to a young Dutchman named Cornelius Boeke. They were married that December, and the wedding turned into a big family reunion, since the Bradleys had just returned from China. They stayed at 'Tennessee' for eight weeks before settling into an English home of their own. The following January Beatrice and Cornelius set out to begin work as missionaries in the Lebanon.

Helen and Charles spent the final months of 1911 at campaigns in a number of towns in the north of Ireland. After this the Chapmans went back to the States for Christmas and the Alexanders returned to 'Tennessee' to set their affairs in order before departing for the forthcoming campaign in Australasia, planned in response to the Australian church leaders' pleas to Charles and Dr Chapman at the end of their last visit that they should return soon.

Helen and Charles and the mission party set out on the long journey to the Antipodes in February 1912, looking forward to meeting old friends 'down under' and to contributing further to the revival that was going on there. Having crossed France, they boarded the S.S. *Otranto* at Toulon. At Naples they were joined by the Chapmans, who had sailed there from New York. While they were there the whole mission party took the opportunity of going to see the fascinating ruins of the Roman city of Pompeii.

The ship reached Australia in early March, having sailed via the Suez Canal and the Indian Ocean. A great welcoming meeting was held for the mission party in the Melbourne Exhibition Building on 11th March. A gruelling programme lay before them, and they knew they could only hope to fulfil all their obligations by the

114

grace of God. They were to attend numerous missions in Australia and New Zealand over a fourteen-month period, with scarcely any time for rest.

The first month was spent in Dunedin in New Zealand, followed by a great campaign in Melbourne and a mission in Adelaide. Then there were five shorter missions in towns all over Australia, each of about a week's duration, followed by a large campaign in Sydney in July and August. Next they attended three missions in smaller towns as they worked their way northwards through Queensland. They then spent two-and-a-half weeks in Brisbane and a few days each at towns along the coast. The final three months in Australia were taken up with campaigns in Victoria and Western Australia. Another three months were then devoted to New Zealand, where they held a series of missions starting at the southern tip of South Island and working up to Auckland at the north of North Island.

A programme such as that would have utterly exhausted Charles and Dr Chapman if they had not been men who depended upon God for their strength and received that strength from heaven in a very real, tangible way. It was absolutely essential to them that they spent time every day praying and meditating upon the Word of God, so that they were always spiritually close to him. They knew that if they did not do this they would quickly become stale and tired in their work and their efforts to win souls to Christ would become mechanical and professional. But this never happened to them, and by the power of the Holy Spirit they were always able to do their work with a divine freshness and genuineness. To them, every conversion they witnessed was thrilling and every testimony of the saving power of God which they heard was exciting.

The evangelists were exposed to constant attention from the press and received the adulation of the crowds everywhere they went, and it would have been easy for men of lesser spiritual stature to be made vain by this, but they never forgot that they were merely the servants of God and never tired of working to bring souls to faith in Christ and to enhance and purify the lives of the churches in the places they visited. In everything they did they tried to focus people's attention not upon themselves but upon the person of the living Lord Jesus Christ.

The campaigns in Australia and New Zealand were immensely successful and did much to fan the flames of revival in the two countries, so when the time came to leave, the mission party had cause to be pleased with their work and to thank God for its effectiveness. They set sail for Vancouver on 10th May 1913 aboard the S.S. *Niagara*. While crossing North America Helen and Charles stopped off at the Moody Bible Institute in Chicago for a few days to meet old friends. They were back at 'Tennessee' on 12th June.

That summer Charles was hard at work in his Den with Robert Harkness and his other musical colleagues, getting ready his third hymn book for use in the campaigns in Glasgow and Edinburgh in the coming autumn and spring. Charles had spent very little time in Scotland since his missions there with Dr Torrey back in 1903 and now hoped to make up for his long absence by bringing blessing and encouragement to the churches there.

Helen was with Charles most of the time throughout these campaigns and took part in the counselling work at the meetings. In January 1914, during a short lull in between the Glasgow and Edinburgh missions, she returned to 'Tennessee' for a few days to entertain some friends there. Having a spare hour on a Sunday afternoon, she took a stroll in the grounds of 'Uffculme', her home before her marriage to Charles. The gardens were full of memories for her – memories of her youth, of the time of grieving she had shared with her mother after her father's death, of Charles' proposal of marriage to her. Then she realised that it was exactly ten years ago to the day that the two of them had taken their first walk together here. He had bared his heart to her and had been overjoyed to discover that she felt about him as he felt about her, and that the Lord was lovingly drawing them together to be man and wife. The past ten years had for both of them been full of excitement and adventure, full of challenge and hard work in God's service and overflowing with reward and blessing from him. The years had also been filled with tender love between she and Charles, interwoven with their deep love for Christ. With a glad, grateful heart Helen returned to 'Tennessee', went to her study and penned this letter to her beloved husband:

It is exactly ten years by the date since you and I wandered round the grounds at Uffculme, alone together for the first time, and passed where the snowdrops were pushing up through the snow. This afternoon I went for a walk round the dear old garden, so altered in many places, but almost the same at that spot, except that the little pool and the summer house, where we sat and talked so sedately, are now shut off by tall iron railings. The snowdrops are coming up in the grass, and I picked a few for 'auld lang syne'. As I stood there in the quiet, I thanked God for all that the ten years have brought us – precious joys and sacred sorrows, wealth of love and friendship, and above all, unique opportunities of winning souls to Christ, of circulating His Word, and of carrying joy and comfort and encouragement to thousands of hearts in many parts of the world through Gospel songs and hymns. Beloved, my heart is too full to utter my thanks to God for you, and for all he has given me in and through you, but He knows that I thank Him 'upon every remembrance' of you. It was about four o'clock as I stood by the snowdrops, so I prayed especially for the men's and women's meetings in Edinburgh, and knew that my prayer was being heard for a great outpouring of the spirit of decision for Christ.

After the conclusion of the Scottish campaigns the Chapmans returned to the States for a while and Helen and Charles spent three glorious weeks together in Cornwall in June and July at Kynance Cove, a quiet spot hidden away between the cliffs about two miles over the moors from Lizard Point. In this wild but lovely place they enjoyed another instalment of the romantic 'honeymoon' which continued through all their years of married life. The love they had had for each other during those six weeks in America after their wedding had never faded, but had grown deeper and more beautiful.

During the summer of 1914 Charles was to a great extent preoccupied with the Pocket Testament League. From the very start it had been his policy to promote it merely as a way of encouraging people to carry the New Testament at all times and to read it daily. He had presented the League as a *method*, and had never intended that it should become a true *organisation* in its own right. However, its worldwide success had been so phenomenal that it had now become necessary for it to be set up on a more formal, permanent footing. By this time it was far too large a movement to remain merely an element of the Chapman–Alexander campaigns. So that summer Charles set up an advisory committee to oversee the work of the League in England during the times when he was abroad.

Another necessity was a central headquarters with a staff wholly dedicated to the League's work, so Charles rented a small upper room in Paternoster Row near St Paul's Cathedral in London. He and Helen furnished it and prayed that God would lead them to the right person to head the operation – someone who was committed to the aims and work of the League and whose life was wholly consecrated to God. Soon he guided them to appoint a Miss E. Wakefield MacGill to the post. She came from Glasgow, was a keen member of the League and had gained invaluable business experience in her previous work. Helen and Charles were not sure what the next step for the League should be, but they had felt strongly guided by God to establish a central organisation and base for it, and so trusted that he would soon make clear the reasons for the guidance he had given. Once the nightmare of the Great War had descended upon Europe, those reasons would become quite plain.

Helen and Charles spent a few days at the Keswick Bible Convention at the end of July and made a flying visit to Scotland in August, during which Charles agreed to take part in a number of missions there in the near future. However, these plans were to be disrupted by the world-shaking events which were soon to take place on the Continent.

When the news of the assassination of the Crown Prince and Princess of Austria reached England, Helen and Charles were entertaining some friends at 'Tennessee'. The atmosphere of Christian fellowship there was as joyful and happy as ever, and although predictions of approaching war had been circulating for the past couple of years, no-one really believed that such a dreadful thing could happen, or that it could affect the peace and security of British life. But the whole nation was about to be swept into the conflict which was soon to rage on the other side of the English Channel.

9

The Nightmare of War

The fateful assassination at Sarajevo in Bosnia created a tense international situation which rapidly escalated into a continent-wide war. Rivalry between the great powers of Europe had been intensifying over recent years, and the killing of the Archduke Francis Ferdinand and his wife proved to be the spark which set the forest alight. Great Britain was obliged to enter the war when the Germans invaded Belgium on 3rd August 1914, since the British had signed a treaty in which they promised to assist Belgium in the event of her being invaded by a foreign power.

So it was that Britain dispatched an Expeditionary Force to France and began recruitment on a massive scale. There was no enlistment as yet, since the widely circulated reports of German atrocities in Belgium had caused great numbers of outraged men to volunteer. Military training camps sprang up all over the country and city streets echoed to the sound of marching. The great expanse of Salisbury Plain rapidly became covered with little cities of white tents. Railway stations were crowded with men and horses bound for the continent or the camps.

Christians throughout the country felt that there was now an urgent job for them to do. The men going to war needed to hear the gospel and receive Christ as their Saviour, because they might soon be facing death, after which they would have no opportunity to repent and believe. Helen and Charles were among those who wanted to do something for the soldiers, and it soon became apparent to them that the Pocket Testament League was an ideal means to this end.

In September came the chance for which they had been hoping and praying. The National Secretary of the British YMCA, which was already doing invaluable service in the camps by setting up canteens providing the men with refreshments and a place in which to spend their leisure time, invited Charles to go to around the camps and sing to the troops. He eagerly rose to the challenge, so with four assistants he went to Salisbury Plain, taking with him thousands of testaments, John's Gospels and hymn books. The soldiers greatly enjoyed the services which he held and made the most of the opportunity to sing and to forget about the harshness of military life. Great numbers of them gladly accepted the testaments and gospels which Charles and his colleagues gave away, each one of them signing the League's pledge to carry his testament everywhere and to read at least a chapter of it every day. As well as the membership pledge the little books also included a straightforward explanation of how a person could become a Christian and selections of Bible verses to help him live the Christian life.

At the end of the first four days of work on Salisbury Plain Charles had seen two thousand men join the League and four hundred accept Christ as their Saviour. This was the beginning of a major effort by the League to bring the gospel to the men going to war, and many willing workers carried on with the task throughout the four year-long conflict, even though Charles was unable to continue with it personally after the autumn of 1914. Over the years to come he was to hear many stories of soldiers and sailors who turned to Christ through reading testaments given to them by the League. It was undoubtedly the case that as a result of the League's work untold thousands killed in action who might otherwise have been destined for a Christless eternity went into the presence of God. Thousands more of those converted through the League's efforts survived the War and lived for Christ in peacetime. This vital ministry in the camps kept Charles very busy that autumn, and many other keen League members also took up the work.

The following was just one of the many stories which Helen and Charles heard about the League's work among the soldiers. A Cornishman named Henry Lane had been eagerly promoting the League in the camps on Salisbury Plain, and over a six-week period had seen an amazing total of three thousand men sign the membership pledge and sixteen hundred receive Christ! One morning at one of the camps a sergeant came up to him and asked him for a Bible or a Testament. Lane asked why he wanted one, and so the sergeant told his story.

The thirty men under his command had been an undisciplined bunch, often drunk, disorderly, insolent and foul-mouthed. At times the sergeant had felt like tearing off his stripes and giving up. However, one night at bedtime one of the men had started reading by the light of a candle.

'What are you reading, mate?' asked one of his comrades.

'I'm reading a Pocket Testament,' the first replied. 'I've joined this thing called the Pocket Testament League, and I've promised to carry this little book with me wherever I go and read a chapter of it every day.'

The other soldiers were slightly taken aback by this and there was silence for a moment. The one of them said, 'Go on, don't be stingy – read us some of it.' So the man read out his day's chapter to the others.

The next day four other men, who had been impressed by the reading from the testament, joined the League, and that night all five men read out their chapters. Eventually every single man in the squad of thirty joined the League and a number of them became Christians. Their behaviour changed dramatically, and disorder and bad language became things of the past. The sergeant was astonished by the transformation he saw taking place among his men and wondered what the cause of it could be. One morning, when he had finished roll-call, the men gathered around him.

'Sergeant, do we have better discipline in our squad now than we used to have?' asked one of them.

'Too right we do!' he agreed.

'Well, do you know what made the difference?' said the private. The men proudly held up their Pocket Testaments. 'This is what did it! We've all joined the Pocket Testament League, and it's changed our lives. It's up to you now, Sergeant. Won't you join us?'

That was his amazing story. 'What could I do, sir,' he said to Lane, 'but come down here and join the League?'

Lane gave him a testament straight away, and he signed the membership pledge. Then he turned to the decision form on the back page and began to explain how the sergeant could become a Christian. He asked him if he would make a decision for Christ there and then.

'Certainly,' replied the soldier. 'I expected to go the whole way today.' And he did.

Because the outbreak of war created an entirely new set of priorities, Charles and Dr Chapman (who had recently returned from the States) had to postpone the planned missions in Scotland and instead concentrated on the work among the camps and on a series of evangelistic meetings in October at the YMCA Head-quarters in Tottenham Court Road in London.

Since they were afterwards due to conduct some campaigns in the States, Charles was now concerned to find someone who could assist Miss MacGill at the Pocket Testament League offices in Paternoster Row. It so happened that Dr J. Louis Fenn, an old friend from Liverpool who had just moved to London to take up the post of rector of a church there, was able to offer his services, and so he was soon appointed as the League's Field Secretary.

On 16th December 1914 Helen and Charles sailed for New York aboard the *Lusitania*. The next few years were to be a trying and testing time for them, since their plans were repeatedly disrupted by the War which, contrary to everyone's initial expectations, turned into a prolonged conflict. As it turned out, they were not to return to 'Tennessee' until after the end of the War, and at times Helen sorely missed her home and her native country. However, throughout this difficult period their faith in God deepened as, facing an uncertain future, they learned to trust more in him and less in their own plans and abilities.

Their first two years in the States were taken up with a long series of Chapman–Alexander campaigns in cities all over the country. Their work continued to be successful and to yield gratifying results. Helen, Charles and the Chapmans usually spent their Saturdays resting, and would often drive out into the country. They went for one these jaunts while they were conducting a mission at Atlanta, Georgia. The countryside bore many resemblances to that of Charles' native state, so he was delighted to be able to return to the surroundings of his boyhood. On their way to see an old-fashioned cotton-gin they passed by a field where an elderly man was laboriously ploughing the earth, using a plough drawn by a mule. On a sudden impulse Charles stopped the car and with a boyish grin jumped out, saying, 'I'd like to see whether I can still plough a straight furrow!' With the old farmer's permission he took the plough handles and urged the mule on, rapidly making a neat, straight furrow in the soil. Then he deftly turned the plough around and made another. Now breathless, he thanked the ploughman and gave him a copy of John's gospel, while from the car Helen and the Chapmans, laughing, loudly applauded his agricultural skill. There were many incidents like this in Helen's marriage to Charles – times when his sheer zest for life would cause him to do something daring or amusing.

One of Helen's most vivid memories of this wartime sojourn in the States was the black people's night held at a campaign in Charlotte, North Carolina. The worship was the most enthusiastic she had ever witnessed. Charles had the time of his life, delighted to be amongst people who loved to praise God every bit as much as he did and who needed no coaxing from him to do it. He greatly valued the black people's instinctive ability to worship God with all their hearts, and often said that white people had a great deal to learn from them in that respect. Indeed, with an exuberant faith like his he felt more at one with black Christians than he did with many white believers, who seemed to have forgotten that the Christians faith was meant to be a joyful way of life – if, indeed, they had ever truly understood that vital truth.

Helen and Charles had planned to return to England in June 1915 and had tentatively booked a passage on the British liner, the *Lusitania*. However, the vessel was sunk by a German submarine off the Irish coast on 7th May because, according to the Germans, she was carrying a cargo of armaments. Because she had been torpedoed without warning, there had been no chance for the passengers to get to the lifeboats, so over eleven hundred of them were drowned. Previously passenger ships had only rarely been attacked, but from now on all transatlantic crossings were considered to be highly dangerous. So the Alexanders had to cancel their plans to return to England, and in fact were not to do so until after the War had ended. Charles and Dr Chapman felt frustrated by this, since they had hoped to be able to do further work in the army camps. However, since they were now obliged to remain in the States, they accepted invitations to appear at a number of Bible conferences there.

A memorable incident occured that summer during a campaign at Springfield, Illinois. At one of the meetings a Dr J. A. Wheeler, Sheriff of Sangamon County, accepted Christ as his Saviour. News of his conversion caused a big stir in his home town, but had an even greater effect upon the jail of which he was in charge. He invited Chapman and Alexander to come to speak to the prisoners, of whom there were a large number. The response was amazing: many of the men were converted, and as a result the whole atmosphere of the jail was changed. Later a number of the converts were baptised at a local church, and went there guarded only by the Sheriff himself. They made no attempt to escape, since they were now determined to respect the law, serve out their sentences and live for Christ in prison. This was just one of countless instances which Helen witnessed of the power of Jesus Christ to radically change human lives.

In February 1916 Helen and Charles, having just arrived in Pittsburg, Pennsylvania, were involved in a serious accident. While they were being taken by a taxi from the railway station to their hotel, the car's steering suddenly failed, and the vehicle crashed into an iron post at the edge of the pavement. Charles was thrown violently onto the glass screen. An artery in his neck was severed and he received bad cuts to his head. Fortunately, one of the best surgeons in Pittsburg happened to live in the hotel they were to stay at, and he was able to deal with Charles' wounds. After two weeks these healed and he made a full recovery. Often in their life together Helen and Charles sensed that they were under attack from evil spiritual forces hostile to their gospel ministry, and sometimes these attacks came in the form of physical mishaps. However, God always protected them in these situations and preserved their lives.

The Pocket Testament League had been launched in the United States in 1908 at Philadelphia, and since that time had spread into many parts of the country, mostly as a result of the Chapman–Alexander campaigns and the tireless efforts of George Davis. However, as had been the case with the League in England in the early days, there was as yet no central headquarters. Just as Charles had felt led by God to set up the office in London, so now he felt irresistibly guided to establish a permanent central base for the League in the States, even though he could not as yet know with certainty why this should be necessary. With hindsight it had become clear that God had prompted him to set up the London office in order that there should be a headquarters for the work that the League was to do in the army camps. Perhaps America was going to enter the War soon, and a similar camp ministry would come into being there.

So Charles rented a large room in the Presbyterian Building on Fifth Avenue in New York City, and soon put Besse D. McAnlis in charge of the operation. She had just graduated from the Bible Institute of Los Angeles and was a keen League member. She took to the appointment with real verve, and within weeks had enlisted into the League a hundred of the people who worked in the Presbyterian Building! It housed dozens of different offices run by various Christian organisations, and their staff were thrilled by Besse's enthusiasm for Christ and his Word. Soon she was holding a daily prayer meeting in her office to which anyone working in the building was welcome to come. The League office rapidly became known as a place for people to go if they wanted to know how to become a Christians or how to lead others to Christ, or if they simply wanted a sympathetic ear and someone to pray with.

Dr Chapman had been suffering from an abdominal problem for some time and now had to undergo two operations. Through much of 1916 he was too ill to work at all, so the joint campaigns which had been planned had to be postponed. However, Charles did take part in a number of small missions of his own during Chapman's period of illness.

In 1917 the USA entered the War on the side of the Allies, and all over the country military training camps sprang up, just as they had done in Britain in 1914.

Very quickly Charles and Dr Chapman (now recovered) became involved in work very similar to that which they had done in the British camps. They rushed from state to state, from camp to camp, bringing the gospel to the men in uniform through song, preaching and the Pocket Testament League.

On 11th November 1918 the Armistice was signed, and the whole world breathed a profound sigh of relief. The nightmare of the past four years was over at last, and everywhere people rejoiced. However, shortly after this Charles and Helen had cause for sadness in their own lives. Dr Chapman's abdominal problem had continued to trouble him intermittently even after his operations, and at the end of December he had to undergo further emergency surgery. He never properly recovered consciousness after this, and eventually passed away very early on Christmas morning. This was a great blow to Charles, because the two men had not only been partners in their work over the past eleven years but had also been the very closest of friends. He had no idea what direction his ministry should take now, but he trusted that God would show the way.

Dr Torrey, his colleague before his association with Chapman, now invited Charles to work with him in a two month-long campaign in Los Angeles in January 1919. Charles accepted gladly. It was a real joy for him to work with Torrey again, and the campaign in Southern California had all the fervour and impact of their joint ministry in the past.

That summer Helen and Charles were at last able to return to England, since they had no further commitments in the States. There had never been a more joyful homecoming at 'Tennessee' than that which took place on 18th July 1919. They were so glad to be back in their own home once again and to be surrounded by the familiar faces of their relatives and their faithful household staff. However, there was also a tinge of sadness about their return because it was so apparent that the nation had passed through deeply traumatic times since their departure at the end of the 1914. And yet there was also much to grateful for. In many ways the country was already starting to recover from the War, although there was a noticeable shortage of men everywhere and those who had returned from the conflict were in many cases finding it difficult to adjust to civilian life. The Cadbury family had been unusually fortunate in that not a single member of it had died in the War, even though Helen's three eldest nephews had been in active service – one in ambulance work, one in the Navy and one in the air service. The latter had narrowly escaped death in a flying accident. Helen was delighted to see how her many nieces and nephews had grown since she was away, although this also made her sad, because she had missed five crucial years of their lives. One of the first things she did on returning was to organise a houseparty for her nieces at 'Tennessee' in September. This was to be the first of many similar happy occasions. That August she and Charles went over to Holland to visit Beatrice and her family. Helen at once fell in love with her four little girls, who chattered away in a mixed dialect of English and Dutch.

Helen and Charles spent the autumn of 1919 and the first weeks of 1920 at a number of Pocket Testament League meetings in England. The League had continued to flourish under the leadership of Miss MacGill and Dr Fenn during the Alexanders' absence.

At the end of January 1920 they sailed for America once more to attend a campaign in Detroit in February and March. This was to be the last major campaign Charles would lead, but it was among the most effective he was ever involved in. It resulted in an astonishing upsurge of interest in the Bible among the people of the city, and the League was very effectively used in achieving this. Charles and Helen were also delighted that during the campaign they were able to see a good deal of Charles's mother and his brother Homer, who now lived together at Trenton, Ohio, a town just twenty-five miles from Detroit.

After the Detroit campaign Charles spent some busy weeks working in Chicago and Philadelphia and appointing a committee of Christian businessmen to look after the League while he was away in England. No one could have then anticipated that they were never to see him again on earth, since he seemed as full of health and energy as ever.

Helen and Charles returned to 'Tennessee' at end of August 1920. Awaiting Charles were numerous invitations to lead campaigns from Christians in Britain, America, Australia and New Zealand, but he felt he had to stay in the United Kingdom for about nine months or a year in order to contribute to the great Bible revival which he believed was imminent, having been inspired by his recent experiences in Detroit. For some reason he did not himself understand he felt unable to make any definite plans beyond the winter of that year, and so made no promises to anyone about his future work.

That September he and Helen enjoyed many wonderful hours together in the new car they had brought back from America, touring in the countryside around Birmingham, visiting places like Worcester, Evesham, Warwick and Stratford-on-Avon. They had never before owned a car in England, and now made the most of the great mobility it gave them. Helen had learned to drive in the States, and loved to be behind the wheel. There were few women drivers in those days, and Charles was proud of his wife's accomplishment. He jokingly called her his 'chauffeur'.

Charles was still feeling somewhat drained after his work in America, so he and Helen started making plans to take a motoring holiday together in Cornwall or North Wales. To most of the people who saw him that summer and autumn he seemed as amazingly full of life as ever, although some – Helen among them – fancied that there was a sort of unearthly radiance about him, as if he were somehow not quite of this world. Everything about him – the peaceful, joyful smile upon his face, the strong, quiet calm in his every movement – seemed to express a closeness to his God greater than he had ever experienced before. The significance of all this was soon to become clear.

The last meeting Charles ever led was a young people's evening at the Friends' Institute in Greet (a suburb of Birmingham) on 28th September. There were only about eighty people present, but this made no difference to Charles, who always put as much of himself into a small meeting as he did into a large one. Everyone in the audience that night joined the Pocket Testament League.

The next day Charles went to Southsea, near Portsmouth, on League business, returning to 'Tennessee' the following afternoon. He was his usual bright, cheery self, but felt extremely tired. That night he was awakened by a sudden heart-attack. A doctor was summoned at once, and after a few hours the pain, which was at first acute, began to ease. By the next day the discomfort had disappeared completely, but he still felt very weak. The doctor was puzzled by this very rapid recovery and wondered whether Charles had indeed suffered a heart attack after all. After a couple of days he was feeling much stronger, and the doctor gave him permission to go for a ride in the country, so long as his wife did the driving. They had several drives together over the next few days, and Charles' condition remained stable, although he lacked his usual strength.

He had promised to act as best man for his old friend and colleague, J.J. Virgo, in Birmingham on Tuesday 12th October. Since it was to be a very quiet wedding, Charles felt he should still fulfil his promise. On the Monday evening Virgo, Charles and Helen enjoyed a happy evening together around the piano at 'Tennessee', singing some favourite old songs and trying out some new ones. Helen was surprised and delighted by Charles' energy that evening, and it seemed scarcely credible that he had been so ill recently. The wedding duly took place they next day without any problems. As she sat at the front of the church watching the ceremony, Helen felt acutely aware of that strange, heavenly beauty and peace surrounding him which she had often sensed over recent weeks. She turned to the friend sitting next to her and asked him if he saw the same thing. 'Yes,' he replied with a sort of gentle awe, 'isn't it wonderful!'

After Charles and Helen had seen the bride and groom off on their honeymoon, they took a stroll together in the gardens of 'Tennessee', making the most of the glorious autumnal sunshine. After admiring the roses they looked in on Charles' young assistants in the Den, who were busily preparing the latest hymn book. Then Helen persuaded Charles to return to the house for a rest, their home being at that time empty of visitors. Usually she loved to have guests about the place, but for some reason she now felt glad that she and her husband could be alone together. The two of them spent a blissful evening, quietly enjoying each other's company and making plans for the time they were to spend with Beatrice, who was due to arrive from Holland the next day for a short visit. They ended their day, as usual, by reading a short passage from the Bible together and praying a few prayers of thanks for the day that was just ending. Then they fell asleep, holding hands. Helen had a strange feeling of dread and held onto Charles' hand tightly.

Then, at about one o'clock in the morning, Charles had another short, sharp attack of pain. His body convulsed and a low moan came from his throat. Helen was instantly wide awake and turned on the bedside light. She saw that although his hand was over his chest, vainly trying to ease the pain, and his face bore an expression of anguish, his eyes were still closed and he seemed not to be awake. Then his hand went limp and his face relaxed into a peaceful smile. With sudden alarm

Helen whispered in his ear: 'Charles are you all right? Wake up, Charles!' But there was no reply. She shook him gently and spoke in his ear again. Still no response. Then she held a hand beneath his nose, but felt no breath upon her palm. She put an ear against his chest, but heard no heartbeat. She ran downstairs to the telephone and called for the doctor, but when he came it was only to confirm that there was nothing he could do.

During their marriage Helen and Charles had on a number of occasions together thought about this test, surely one of the hardest in life: the test of being left alone. They had realised that one of them would have to face it after the other had gone into the presence of God. Often in recent days Helen had cried out in prayer, 'Not that test, O Lord – spare me that test!' But the heavenly Father had now in his wisdom allowed her to suffer the test, and with faith and courage she had to confront it.

Once the doctor had gone Helen asked the servants to leave the bedroom for a while, and then she shut the door. In her heart of hearts she had been expecting Charles' death. The first heart attack and that strange, heavenly quality which had hung about him recently had hinted that his departure was imminent, but she had still hoped and prayed with all her heart that her husband would remain with her for many years. Perhaps in the deepest part of his soul Charles, too, had known what was to come, and for that reason had made no plans for the future. Now that the unwelcome parting had taken place, Helen knew that it was meant to be, and so although heartbroken she was not in a state of shock. She could respond to what had happened with faith.

She knelt beside the bed where her beloved husband lay, tears streaming down her face. She gave thanks to God that his passing had been so easy for him, since the second heart attack had done its work without awakening him. She was also thankful that he would never have to face the test that was now hers. Most of all she gave thanks that he was now in the presence of the Saviour whom he had loved and served with all his heart. She felt no sorrow for him – rather, he was greatly blessed. 'Father in heaven,' she prayed, 'please give me strength to live without Charles – enable me to live to glorify you, and as Charles would have wanted me to live.'

Immediately God's promise to the Apostle Paul came into her mind as if someone in the room had said it aloud: '*My grace is sufficient for thee.*' She knew that God had spoken to her in her need. With trembling lips she humbly prayed: 'with your grace, Father, I will not fail you – or him!' Then she felt a wonderful peace flooding every part of her being – as assurance that God would care for her, provide for her and sustain her in every way.

She raised her head and gazed at the body of her husband. The gentle, joyful smile which had been upon his lips at his dying moment was still there. She knew that his spirit had seen that he was passing from life's struggle into perfect rest in God's presence. She sat on the edge of the bed and took his hand, now cold, in hers. 'Goodbye, Charles, my love,' she said, and kissed him on his lips for the last time. But she knew that this was not a final farewell, and that they would meet again in the life to come. On a sudden, loving impulse she put the little testament which she had carried with her for years into his right hand and closed his fingers around it. That was how he would have wanted his body to be laid to rest – clutching the precious Word of God which he had read and believed and preached and promoted throughout a life dedicated to the Lord. As Helen looked upon his face she remembered that the Bible said, 'Eye hath not seen, nor ear heard, neither hath entered into the heart of man, the things which God hath prepared for them that love him.' Helen knew that now Charles was enjoying the privilege of seeing those things.

The atmosphere which reigned in the Alexander home in the days following Charles' death was not a gloomy one. There was an air of reverence, because with his death heaven had in a way come into the house, but there was no morbid grieving. Charles had gone to be with his Saviour, and that was a cause for rejoicing and celebration. Those who loved him – Helen above all – would miss him painfully, but they did not permit themselves to selfishly wish that he were still with them.

Charles' body was to be laid to rest on the morning of Saturday 16th October. A small group of family and friends came to 'Tennessee' before the funeral and gathered around the simple oak casket in which the body lay. It bore no decoration other than a brass plate bearing Charles' signature – so familiar to them all from the innumerable warm and friendly letters he had written in his life – and the 'II Timothy 2:15' Scripture reference which he had always put beneath his name. The verse read: 'Study to show thyself approved unto God, a workman that needeth not be to ashamed, rightly dividing the word of truth.' It had been the motto of his life, and there was no doubt in the mind of anyone present that morning that he had lived up to it. This workman had most certainly pleased his heavenly Master.

Charles had never gone to any sort of public meeting without first committing it to God, and they all knew that he would have wanted this morning to be no exception to that rule, so before setting out for the cemetery they spent a short time in prayer.

Funerals were not allowed at Lodge Hill Cemetery on Saturday afternoons, so the ceremony had to be held in the morning. This unfortunately meant that many of those who would have dearly loved to come were unable to reach the place in time, so the mourners, although numbering over three hundred, were by no means as numerous as they would otherwise have been. They gathered around the grave of Helen's and Charles' short-lived son, in which his father's body was also to be buried.

The coffin was carried respectfully upon the shoulders of six friends. Close behind came Helen, with Beatrice at her side, followed by many members of the Cadbury family. Then came Miss MacGill and Dr Fenn, representing the Pocket Testament League, and numerous friends. Among them was Wilbur T. Gracey, the American consul in Birmingham, who was officially representing the government and people of the United States, great numbers of whom had known and loved their fellow-countryman Charles Alexander.

Dr Fenn led the simple graveside service, which began with *The sands of time are sinking,* one of Charles' favourite hymns. Then a number of Bible passages chosen by Helen were read out, after which her brother Richard and Beatrice led the people in prayer. Helen's uncle George said a few words in memory of Charles and Dr Fenn gave the closing message, emphasising the threefold passion of Charles' life – a passion for Christ, for his Word and for souls – and appealing to those present who had not yet given their lives to Christ to do so that day. There was another hymn, and a few moments of silence. Then Helen prayed aloud briefly, even though she had not planned to do so, thanking God for the sixteen years of heaven upon earth which she had had with Charles. Those who heard her were amazed at the strength she was showing in the face of her bereavement, and it was apparent to all that God was the source of that strength. Then the crowd slowly dispersed while some local Christian young people sang the *Glory song.* The words were highly poignant and appropriate:

> When by the gift of his infinite grace,
> I am accorded in heaven a place,
> Just to be there and look on his face,
> Will through the ages be glory for me.

The funeral was just as Charles would have wanted it. Above all he would have wanted his passing away to be used as an opportunity for bringing other people to faith in Christ. The message given by Dr Fenn challenged a number of mourners to consider commitment to Christ, and some of the other League members present spoke to the coachmen and taxi-drivers who had brought people to the cemetery. May of them gladly received testaments and five received Christ there and then. In the next few days the League gained many more members among the undertakers and other people connected with the funeral.

Three days later Helen and Beatrice went back to the cemetery to lay some roses at the grave at the cabled request of Charles' mother in America. They then called at the lodge to thank the head gardener for the kind and thoughtful way in which he had made he arrangements for the burial. Helen knew him, since he had previously been the gardener at Moseley Hall during her childhood. She got into conversation with him and was surprised to discover that he had never definitely accepted Christ as his Saviour. However, he had been moved by Charles' funeral and after a few words with Helen took that step of faith and accepted a testament. His wife was with them and also committed herself to Christ. It was a wonderful encouragement to Helen amidst the sadness of losing Charles that his dying had been the means of bringing others into eternal life. A letter from her eldest sister Jessie expressed well what she herself felt: 'It has been a great, heart-stirring time . . . This passing can only be called a triumph over death. It had lifted many into the sunshine of heaven.'

On the Wednesday after the funeral a service of praise and testimony in memory of Charles was held at the Central Hall in Birmingham and was attended by about twelve hundred people. Many Christians there, inspired by the example of his life, dedicated themselves to Christ with a renewed zeal.

Over the coming weeks Helen received many hundreds of letters of condolence from those who had known and loved Charles. Like her, they were struggling to come to terms with the realisation that they would never again on earth hear his merry laugh or his beautiful, passionate singing, and they would never again see his sunny, joyful smile. But many of them shared with Helen an inner assurance that at the Resurrection they would be reunited with him. A letter from an American friend read:

I was surprised to hear of the passing of Mr Alexander. He seemed to be so full of vitality and strength, that somehow I never associated the thought of death with him. I know of no one, however, who gave me a more genuine impression of being heartily at home in both worlds, and I know how full of eager interest he would be in all the great discoveries of the new experience. There was so much for him to do here, and his capacity for friendship and companionship was so great, that his friends are deeply grieved; and yet I know there are many people to whom heaven will be a more home-like place because he is there.

With a heart aching for Charles but full of trust in her God, Helen now turned her thoughts towards the future, determined to live and work for Christ with all her heart, in whatever way he chose for her.

10

Helen's later life

With Charles' death, Helen again experienced the sensation of loss and loneliness which she had known after the departure of her beloved father. If anything the pain of separation was even worse now, because there is no closer relationship in life than that between husband and wife, and that bond had now been broken, never to be repaired. Moreover, theirs had been no ordinary marriage, and through their mutual love for Christ they had grown closer than many couples do. He had given them a deeper and stronger love for each other than they could ever have had without him. Charles had not been the centre of Helen's life, for Christ himself had always held that place, but she and her husband had been like two planets orbiting the same sun, and now her orbit seemed strangely unbalanced without her companion. And yet the same God who had given such life and strength to their marriage now drew close to Helen in her bereavement as she drew closer to him than ever before, in her heart trusting that he would show her how to go on living.

She had always been a highly energetic woman and had never willingly been idle, and so she now busied herself by working for the Pocket Testament League and visiting the many members of her family and entertaining them at 'Tennessee'. She also spent her time writing a lengthy and very readable biography of her beloved Charles. As the years went by she got over the initial pain of her bereavement, but as long as she lived she never ceased to miss him.

The thought of remarriage had been far from Helen's mind, and so she was most surprised to receive a proposal while she was in the States in 1923. The suitor was Dr Amzi Clarence Dixon, one of Charles' many American friends and an evangelist of international repute who from 1911 to 1919 had been the pastor of the Metropolitan Tabernacle in London, formerly the church of the famous preacher Charles Haddon Spurgeon. Helen and Clarence had got to know each other well, but she was still somewhat shocked by his proposal. She felt that although they were friends, he was overstepping the mark in presuming that she might consider marrying again, and so at first she politely refused him. However, eventually she came to agree with him that they had much in common. They had both been widowed, and so understood each other's grief, and they shared a zeal for evangelistic work. Before long she came to feel as he did that God was drawing them together to comfort and support each other and to share in the work of bringing souls to Christ.

They had a quiet wedding in London on 25th January 1924. Helen was now aged forty-seven and Clarence was seventy. They enjoyed a ten day-long honeymoon in Cornwall, Helen's favourite part of England. 'Tennessee' was their permanent home, but Clarence's preaching work kept them in Europe and North America for much of the time. However, the marriage was a short-lived one, since in July 1925 Clarence died of cancer of the spine. Once again Helen was alone, and after the shock of her second husband's death definitely decided that she would never remarry. She had known three wonderful Christian men in her lifetime – her father, Charles and Clarence – and that was enough for her.

She spent most of the remainder of her life in England at 'Tennessee', busily involved with various Christian organisations – especially the Pocket Testament League, of course. She never lost her enthusiasm for sharing the gospel message with others. She had a meeting hall built

140

next to the old Tea Sheds and there every Saturday one Christian group or another would gather, provided with refreshments by her household staff. Helen was a familiar figure to many people, standing at the gate of her home to welcome her visitors.

One of the most remarkable activities in which she was involved in her later life was helping to bring quite a number of Jews out of Germany and Austria shortly before the start of the Second World War. Thanks to her and those she worked with, they escaped death at the hands of the Nazis.

She nearly always had guests staying at 'Tennessee', either relatives or missionaries from overseas. Every one of them had to sign her Visitors' Book, which by the end of her life was many volumes long, containing the signatures of Christian people from every corner of the globe.

Mealtimes at 'Tennessee' were entertaining occasions. Helen would sit at the head of the table and talk with her guests, always keen to hear about their experiences and to share hers with them. Even when very elderly she kept her quick wits and remained an accomplished conversationalist and storyteller. Most of all she loved to talk about her beloved Charles and the fascinating trips to Egypt she had had with her father when she was a girl.

Her guests were often amazed and quietly amused by the importance she attached to protocol at meals. The food had to be served and eaten in exactly the right way. Often she would correct her young relatives when they were doing something wrong, even when they were mature adults! They had to sit up straight in their chairs and keep their elbows off the table. 'All joints on the table will be carved,' she would say jokingly. However, the warmth and genuineness of her love and the liveliness of her sense of humour and fun more than made up for her fussiness at the table.

Being in the Cadbury family, she still had connections with the chocolate-making business, although she was not directly involved in it in any way. Often guests at 'Tennessee' would be taken to see the famous factory at Bournville and at the end of their stays at Helen's home would be weighed down with boxes of chocolates!

She had few regrets about her life, but the one she felt most keenly was her inability to have any more children after the death of her short-lived son in 1911. However, she made up for this a little by lavishing her strong maternal affection upon her young relatives. They all had very fond memories of their aunt (or great-aunt) Helen.

To her last day Helen displayed the amazing energy which had been a hallmark of her character throughout her life. Assisted by her faithful household staff (many of whom remained with her until their retirement), she ran 'Tennessee' with astonishing efficiency and attention to detail. In accordance with her wishes expressed in her will, after her death the house was converted into a home for the elderly, especially those who had been involved in Christian work.

She never lost her youthful love of music and retained a fine singing voice well into her old age, continuing to sing in one of the local choirs until she was ninety! She especially loved to sing songs from the hymnals which Charles had published. They brought back to her many happy memories of the fascinating and exciting life she had led with him. She was always in love with him, and until her dying day kept his Den, with its innumerable papers, books and lantern slides, just as it had been when he was alive. Of course, she had had a great fondness for Clarence, but Charles remained the real love of her life.

In her later life she developed arthritis and had to undergo a hip replacement operation. However, she bore the pain and inconvenience of this with the courage and energy which was so typical of her, and even though she afterwards had to get about using sticks for support, it hardly seemed to slow her down at all! The arthritis prevented her from driving any more, but she remained passionately fond of cars, particularly American ones. Her chauffeur, Day, who was in her employment for many years, became one of her closest friends. She also suffered a stroke in her old age, but recovered from it very well.

Of course, Helen always retained a very keen interest in the Pocket Testament League, of which she was the Founder and International President until her death, and never lost the healthy habit of carrying her pocket testament with her everywhere. During her lifetime the rapid growth of the organisation continued and its work spread into many countries. By 1936 it had a total of five million members worldwide. During the Second World War the League did work among the armed services similar to that which it had done during the previous conflict, distributing great numbers of testaments. The USA branch alone gave away over two million of them. After the War the League sent a million New Testaments to Taiwan, half a million Testaments and fifteen million Gospels to Japan and two hundred thousand Testaments to Germany. A big event in Helen's later life was her trip to the States in November 1957 to attend the dedication service at the newly completed headquarters building of the American arm of the League in Englewood, New Jersey.

Over the years the League has become more than a scripture distribution agency and has evolved into a missionary organisation. Today it has evangelists in Brazil, Mexico, India, Indonesia, the Philippines, Australia, Portugal, Spain, France, Italy, Holland, Belgium, Germany and the USA as well as in the United Kingdom. In Brazil Ron and Esther Milligan and other evangelistic teams have distributed over ten million Gospels of John. Father-and-son team Daniel and David Poysti, based in Germany, are supplying Bibles and Gospels to Russia, Poland, Yugoslavia and Hungary.

Daniel's brother Earl and his family are producing evangelistic radio programmes in Russian.

One of the League's major projects in recent years has been the reaching of China with the gospel. After the Communist takeover in 1949 it was difficult to get Christian literature into the country, so for some years the League beamed a daily radio programme onto the Chinese mainland. When the restrictions were finally lifted, hundreds of thousands of gospels were sent to individuals who asked for them.

Helen Cadbury died peacefully on 1st March 1969 at 'Tennessee', aged ninety-two. The little group which she had formed in her school days had grown into an organisation serving God all over the world. Who can estimate the number of people who have put their faith in Christ and have grown into mature believers through reading Bibles, Testaments and Gospels supplied to them by the Pocket Testament League? The true figure must run into many millions. Today the League's workers around the globe continue to carry out their vital task, because the Word of God still has the power to change people's lives.

Further information about the Pocket Testament League's present work can be obtained from this address: Cosmos House, 6 Homesdale Road, Bromley, Kent BR2 9LZ.

Bibliography

Helen Cadbury, *Richard Cadbury of Birmingham*, Hodder and Stoughton, London, 1906.

Helen Cadbury Alexander and J. Kennedy Maclean, *Charles M. Alexander: A Romance of Song and Soul-Winning*, Marshall Brothers, London (undated).

Helen C. A. Dixon, *A. C. Dixon: A Romance of Preaching*, G. P. Putnam's Sons, New York, 1931.

Leslie James, *The Quaker Girl and Her League*, Pocket Testament League, Bromley, 1986.

Iain Murray, *The Forgotten Spurgeon,* Banner of Truth Trust, London, 1966.

Vision and Venture 1949-55, the Pocket Testament League's quarterly magazine.